Contents

Acknowledgements

We would like to thank all the parents and children at Pen Green who contributed to this book in so many different ways. We'd also like to express our gratitude to the rest of the staff at the Centre who encouraged us to finish this book so that we could get on with our day job, i.e. working with children and families! Special thanks go to Colette Tait for deciphering and interpreting and finally typing up all our contributions and to Ellen Burgess for all her hard work taking photographs.

We also want to acknowledge a huge debt of gratitude to Chris Athey, Research Fellow, and Tina Bruce, Teacher, whose inspirational work on the Early Education Project at the Froebel Institute influenced all of us. This project gave early childhood educators throughout the United Kingdom a new vision of how it is possible to work with parents in a partnership which can change children's lives.

Working with PARENTS

MARGY WHALLEY

THE PEN GREEN CENTRE TEAM

Hodder & Stoughton

A MEMBER OF THE HODDER HEADLINE GROUP

Dedication

This book is dedicated to Tasha, my amazing seventeen year old daughter who has taught me so much about being a parent.

Orders: please contact Bookpoint Ltd, 130 Milton Park, Abingdon, Oxon OX14 4SB. Telephone: (44) 01235 827720, Fax: (44) 01235 400454. Lines are open from 9.00–6.00, Monday to Saturday, with a 24 hour message answering service. Email address: orders@bookpoint.co.uk

British Library Cataloguing in Publication Data
A catalogue record for this title is available from The British Library

ISBN 0 340 688130

First published 1997
Impression number   11   10   9   8   7
Year   2005   2004

Hodder Headline's policy is to use papers that are natural, renewable and recyclable products and made from wood grown in sustainable forests. The logging and manufacturing processes are expected to conform to the environmental regulations of the country of origin.

Typeset by Wearset, Boldon, Tyne and Wear.
Printed in Great Britain for Hodder & Stoughton Educational, a division of Hodder Headline Plc, 338 Euston Road, London NW1 3BH by J. W. Arrowsmith Ltd, Bristol.

Notes on contributors

MARGY WHALLEY – EDITOR

Margy Whalley has a seventeen year old daughter and has worked for over twenty years in education and care settings in Britain, Brazil and Papua New Guinea. She is a qualified teacher with an MA in Community Education and she is currently directing a research programme at the Pen Green Centre concerned with 'Parents' Involvement in their Children's Learning'.

KATEY MAIRS

Katey Mairs has been head of an education and care setting for many years. She is a qualified teacher with wide experience in both inner city and community nurseries and jointly financed combined centres. She is an outstanding practitioner with a deep commitment to involving parents in the nursery setting.

CATH ARNOLD

Cath Arnold is a senior teacher in an education with care setting. She has over twenty years' experience within private and public sector day care and educational provision. She qualified as a licensed teacher five years ago and is currently undertaking research towards a Master's Degree in Education. Her research interests are parents' involvement in their children's learning and the patterns in children's play.

MARGARET MYLES

Margaret Myles holds the NVQ Level 3 in Childcare and has undertaken advanced counselling training. She has many years of experience working with very disadvantaged and hard to engage parents. She works with particularly vulnerable children from age 18 months to three years. She has been very involved in setting up and running a parent education group in a family centre.

BERNADETTE CAFFREY

Bernie Caffrey works as Assistant Head of School of Health Care and Science at Tresham Institute, a college of further and higher education. Bernie teaches and assesses on early years training courses and acts as an Internal Verifier for NVQs in Childcare and Education. She has a nursing, midwifery and health visiting background.

ANGELA MALCOLM

Angela Malcolm is a senior family worker in an education and care setting. She has many years' experience of working directly with parents and children in a multi-disciplinary setting. She completed the DPQS and has the teacher's certificate for working with adult learners. She has run a very successful ALBSU (BSA) project for several years and has written up and presented her work at a number of conferences, both nationally and internationally.

DI BREWSTER

Di Brewster has many years' experience working in social services family centres and in combined education and care centres, supporting parents with young children. She is committed to encouraging and working with parents who want to be involved in adult community education, adult literacy and numeracy programmes. Di has been a single parent to four children since 1978.

MAXINE MCKAY

Maxine McKay has four children and has been involved with the Pen Green Centre for ten years as a parent. She has completed a range of vocational and non-vocational courses at the Centre, most recently the NVQ Level 3 in Working with Children and Families. She has undertaken training in groupwork and in aromatherapy and massage. She now runs a number of groups at the Centre for parents and babies.

LUCY RUSSELL

Lucy Russell is a family worker and co-ordinator for children with special educational needs. She holds the NNEB qualification and has completed counselling training at an advanced level at the University of North London. She has run a support group for parents with children with special educational needs for three years.

TREVOR CHANDLER

Trevor Chandler is a principal social worker with two young children. He has worked with children's psychological services and in social work settings. He has managed an early childhood service for nine years and has published and lectured widely on the role of men in childcare services and on fathers' involvement in the nursery.

MARCUS DENNISON

Marcus Dennison is a family worker in an education with care setting. He holds the NVQ Level 3 in Working With Children and Families and is the father of three young children. He has lectured on involving men in childcare and on the role of the family worker as a key worker.

DONNA VIZMA

Donna Vizma has an Open University degree in Combined Studies. She is an experienced community educator. She has run a women returners project in an early childhood setting for four years. She also has considerable experience in co-ordinating an NVQ programme in a combined nursery centre.

Bernadette Caffrey

Di Brewster

Lucy Russell

Katey Mairs

Margy Whalley

Angela Malcolm

Marcus Dennison

Margaret Myles

Maxine McKay

Cath Arnold

Trevor Chandler

Donna Vizma

All practitioners in the nursery
share the same underlying
principles

Introduction

Services need to be planned and delivered in order to respond to . . . individual needs. Services must not be delivered in inflexible packages or be based on a stereotype of families' needs and priorities. These have to be discussed and negotiated (UN, 1994).

This book has been written by a group of practitioners with a range of experience in early childhood education, care and social services and further education settings. All the contributors have worked with parents at Pen Green and elsewhere over a period of time. As early years practitioners we have had to carve time out of our hectic schedules to write since most of us are combining working with parents and children with being parents to our own children at home. We've tried to focus on the role of the early childhood educator as a resourceful friend to both parents and children. We are all committed to creating an environment within the local community where **all** parents with young children would feel equally welcomed and valued. It's clear to us that parents have a critical role to play in their children's learning and development. Young children achieve more and are happier when early years educators work together with parents.

Bringing experience from a wide range of settings, we have worked together with parents to create Pen Green, a neighbourhood centre for young children and their families in Corby, Northamptonshire. It is a new kind of service combining:

- ▶ early years education
- ▶ flexible daycare for children in need and children with special educational needs
- ▶ parent education and support for parents
- ▶ community health services
- ▶ training and support for early years practitioners
- ▶ research and development.

Each chapter in this book reflects the views and value base, the training and experience and the deep personal interest of the individual contributor. When we met to plan and work on this book we took time to discuss the underlying principles behind our work, which we felt should be common to every chapter. These are the principles that all the contributors share and which are fundamental to the way we work with parents.

> ▶ We believe in parents' commitment to their children.
> ▶ We want to share power with parents and work in an enabling way.
> ▶ We want our service to be equally accessible to all parents and know that we have to continually challenge our practice to achieve this.
> ▶ We believe that parents need to have a choice of services.
> ▶ We know that a 'blaming' approach doesn't work and is inappropriate. Parents generally want the best for their children.
> ▶ We know that we should respect parents' culture and context and avoid stereotyping parents.
> ▶ We believe that we shouldn't work in isolation: we need to create networks with other people and organisations.
> ▶ We know that **we** will need to be flexible and adaptable – if we want to work with parents we should not be asking parents to do all the adapting.
> ▶ Whilst we all need training and support we believe that the best way to learn as an early years educator is to ask parents to teach us.

Bibliography

UN, (1944) Families & Disability. Occasional Papers Series No. 10. Vienna: United Nations.

1

Working with Parents in Early Childhood Settings

Parents and professionals can help children separately or they can work together to the greater benefit of the children (Athey, 1990).

In this chapter the reasons and rationale behind this book are considered. We reflect on **why** early years practitioners in the new millennium will need to work closely with parents as well as young children. In order to do this the history and development of education and care services in this country are briefly outlined. We look at **who** the parents are that we are engaging in our different kinds of services. We also describe **how** early years educators can establish a positive dialogue with parents and develop an equal and active partnership with them. Throughout this book the term 'parents' is used to represent the children's principal care givers. Clearly there may be a number of important adults in a child's life and these may or may not be his or her biological parents.

Why work with parents?

If you've just finished your training you may be thinking, 'I came into early years education and care because I wanted to work with young children – why do I need to work with their parents?'

If you have already been working for some time in an early years setting providing exciting and stimulating services for babies, toddlers and young children whilst their parents work you may wonder, 'how relevant is this book going to be to my setting?'

If you are working in a nursery school or nursery class or playgroup where parents are already involved in helping in the classroom or in running sessions perhaps you're thinking, 'there's not a lot that we could do differently.'

The first nurseries

The first nursery education and day care services which were set up in this country nearly a hundred years ago included programmes for involving parents. Margaret McMillan who set up open air nurseries for children living in poverty at the beginning of the twentieth century strongly believed that the only way to bring about change in society was to combine nursery education and parent education. She thought that staff in nursery schools and day care centres should take action to:

> ▶ support and educate little children
> ▶ educate parents, encouraging them to take control of early years services and their lives.

Margaret McMillan was clear that both kinds of action needed to happen in our nurseries if any real change was to take place in a society where many families were destitute.

Her radical early years programmes included lectures for parents by some of the most famous contemporary politicians and educationalists. She also encouraged nurseries to set up parents' groups.

Every nursery school should have its mothers' club. Ours is held weekly. The mothers join so as to be part of a new movement, a movement that has already changed to some degree their own lives and the lives of their children (Margaret McMillan, quoted in Lowndes, 1960).

Losing the spirit of Margaret McMillan

It wasn't until the 1960s that taking action to involve parents once again became a focus for work in early years education and care services. This time the radical element that had been present in Margaret McMillan's work was lost. It became fashionable in the United Kingdom and the USA to set up parent intervention programmes in areas of poverty where children's achievement seemed to be low. The idea was that nursery schools, nursery classes, and day nurseries needed to compensate for what children weren't getting at home. Parents, which generally meant mothers, were encouraged to come into the early years settings so that they could be taught how to 'play' more effectively with their young children. Parents were seen as inept and in need of expert guidance from professionals who had all the skills and expertise.

Although the projects that were set up in the 1960s and 1970s were often described as being about a partnership between professionals and parents, the partnership was not equal. The professionals had all the power. **They** decided what services should be offered, how they should be offered and where they were delivered. The parents were not actively engaged in making decisions about the kinds of services being offered or the nature of their involvement.

At this time there was an assumed set of skills that parents needed to be taught if their children were going to achieve more in school. Few professionals seemed to recognise the skills and experiences that parents already had. There was very little understanding of the role of the parents as their children's first educator. The focus of these programmes was very much on what children **weren't** able to do rather than on children's competencies and strengths.

Think about a child that you know who is struggling in your nursery setting. You **could** start by describing what he can't do and what he doesn't know, like this:

> Tom isn't toilet trained yet and wet himself twice in nursery today. He doesn't know how to share and is constantly snatching things from the other children and he is hardly ever indoors.

Both Tom and his parents might find it easier to recognise Tom from this alternative description of his behaviour, which emphasises what he **can** do.

> Tom is new to nursery and is particularly interested in the water wheel. He shows a great deal of persistence. He stays outside even when it is quite cold and is learning how to make the water flow over the water wheel. He is so excited by his discoveries that he finds it hard to share with other children and needs to have his right to play alone supported by nursery staff. Sometimes he's so excited he forgets to run to the toilet but when he does have an accident he handles it really well. He knows how to undo his trouser buttons and always goes to a member of staff for help.

In the same way we **could** comment on what the parents **aren't** doing:

Karen's mum never bothers to come to parents' evenings. Karen really doesn't concentrate on anything very much in nursery and it seems like no-one at home takes any interest.

Alternatively, we could look at what Karen's parents **are** doing to educate and support their children:

Mrs Devlin comes to pick up Karen from nursery every day even though she has difficulty getting the twins' double buggy through the nursery entrance. She always encourages Karen to take a book home from the book box. Everybody in Karen's family is suffering a bit this month as the twins are teething and keeping them all awake.

The parenting programmes in the 1960s and 1970s often failed to recognise the difficulties some parents faced just getting into their children's schools or nurseries. Many parents would have previously experienced rejection and failure in the school system. For those parents it would have been hard to see school buildings as friendly or welcoming places. Even when parents were motivated to attend courses and training events they might well have experienced practical problems both in getting to the setting and in committing themselves to a regular programme. These practical constraints might make it difficult for parents to attend:

> ▶ pressure of work
> ▶ no transport to get to the setting
> ▶ living on a low income and needing to do part-time work as it becomes available
> ▶ needing to pick up older children from schools
> ▶ lack of crèche facilities for babies and toddlers
> ▶ no support at home and the pressure of housework and childcare.

When these parent involvement programmes failed to work some professionals assumed that it was because parents just didn't care. Others thought that it was because parents didn't understand how important it was that they should get involved in their children's education and development. They assumed that parents didn't see the relevance of a partnership with schools.

The way ahead

If parents are to be effectively supported in early years settings then a very different working model needs to be adopted. We need to acknowledge the fact that:

> Parents are the most important people in their children's lives. It is from parents that children learn most, particularly in the early months and years . . . the closer the links between parent and nursery . . . the more effective that learning becomes (RSA, 1994).

It must be recognised, as highlighted by Margaret McMillan, that poverty not apathy is one of the biggest problems for many parents with children under five.

A real partnership with parents involves power-sharing, a recognition of parents' equally valuable knowledge and expertise and an understanding of the real pressures that young families face. Projects that aim to do things to parents are generally much less effective than projects where parents are **intrinsically motivated** – where they are doing things for themselves. There must be a strong and explicit value base, preferably one that is spelt out in all our documents, booklets and policy statements. What we as staff in nurseries personally believe about children's rights and the rights of parents will inevitably affect the way we work. As a staff group we will need to negotiate a set of values that we can all share and own in our work.

A value base

A value base is usually negotiated and discussed with staff over a number of years. At Pen Green nursery staff believe in certain values.

> ▶ **Parents and children both have rights.** We live in a society where parents get very little practical support (Social Justice Strategies for National Renewal 1994 The Report of the Commission on Social Justice). Increasing numbers of children are being brought up in poverty, and services to support families are not logically or fairly distributed. We need to find a balance so that both parents and children get what they want from our services. Services need to be equally accessible to **all** parents and children.

▶ **Being a parent is a complex and difficult role,** and not one for which any of us is 'trained'. Most people experience some difficulties while they are trying to become competent parents. Many lose their confidence and would welcome some support for what can often become a lonely and demanding job.

> Parenting is **not** simply an aggregate of skills, though some skills can be learnt, but it is a unique relationship between two individuals (Puckering, 1994).

▶ **Parenting is a key concern for both men and women** – it isn't a 'mother's issue'. Fathers also have rights and responsibilities as parents. Parent programmes need to involve and meet the needs of fathers, as well as mothers.

▶ **In our early years centres we must create a culture of high expectations.**

- Parents have a right to expect high quality, flexible services that respond to the changing needs of their families.
- Staff need to believe in parents' deep commitment to supporting their children's learning. They need to encourage parents to increase their competence.
- Parents and staff both need to have high expectations of the children. They need to work together to get children the best possible deal.

Once you have an **agreed value base** within your early years setting then those values need to be translated into the way you work directly with parents and their children.

How values translate into practice

If you believe that both parents and children have rights then you will want to create spaces in your setting which are 'parent-friendly' (assuming your setting will already be offering an exciting provision for children). These parent-friendly spaces will need to look and feel very different from a conventional classroom environment. There will need to be room for adult-sized chairs, appropriate facilities for making tea and coffee at a safe height well away from children, books, magazines and play equipment for younger children. Staff from the setting, workers from other organisations or volunteers will need to be there with time to listen to parents.

Throughout this book you will discover many examples of staff with different backgrounds and experience using these agreed values in their direct work with parents. If you want to see how these values work in relation to involving fathers then you may want to turn straight to chapter 9. If you're concerned about working with parents when their children are on the Child Protection Register and the family is experiencing a lot of vulnerability then chapter 4 will offer you some concrete suggestions. If you're particularly interested in working with parents who have a child with special educational needs then you may want to start with chapter 8.

Remember that unlike documents within your setting which have to be constantly updated your statement of values and principles should endure over many years. It will, however, be important for you to renegotiate your statement of values every time you appoint a new member of staff. Everyone in your setting has to agree and own a particular way of working with parents which is underpinned by your value base. It's no good having an agreed way of working if, in practice, half the staff are doing something different! When new parents or visitors from outside your setting come round to see what's going on it will be very obvious to them that there is a consistent way of working which is based on a shared belief system.

Parents as partners

The School Curriculum and Assessment Authority in 1996 recognised the need for **all** early years establishments to work more closely with parents. They issued some 'desirable outcomes' guidelines. These stated that:

> ► Parents' fundamental role in their child's education is acknowledged by staff in the setting and a partnership, based on shared responsibility, understanding, mutual respect and dialogue, is developed.
> ► There is recognition of the role parents have already played in the early education of their child and that their continued involvement is crucial to successful learning.
> ► Parents feel welcome and there are opportunities for collaboration among parents, staff and children.
> ► There is recognition of the expertise of parents and other adults in the family and this expertise is used to support the learning opportunities provided within the setting.
> ► Adults working in the setting give parents access to information about the curriculum in a variety of ways, e.g. open days, meetings, social events, brochures and video presentations (in different languages where appropriate).

> ▶ Parents contribute to and are fully informed of their child's progress and achievements.
> ▶ Admission procedures are flexible to allow time for discussion with parents and for children to feel secure in the new setting.
> ▶ Opportunities for learning provided in the setting are sometimes continued at home, e.g. reading and sharing books, and experiences initiated at home are sometimes used as stimuli for learning in the setting.

When early years settings are inspected by OFSTED the inspectors will be looking for these key features to be present (see list of 'desirable outcomes'). When **all** early years settings demonstrate these key features then partnership with parents will become a reality.

In settings where early years educators are already working in an exciting and creative partnership with parents then they may want to build on these 'desirable outcomes' and offer a range of direct services that support parents in their important role.

Who are the parents?

When we use the term 'parents' we are using a shorthand. We are actually referring to all the important adults in a child's life. Sometimes these important adults are the child's biological parents but the term refers here to any other adults who are involved in caring for and bringing up the children in our early years settings.

As their primary carers children may have:

> ▶ a single-parent mother
> ▶ a single-parent father
> ▶ two parents, the biological mother and father living in a heterosexual relationship
> ▶ two working parents
> ▶ two parents from minority ethnic groups
> ▶ a single parent who is working
> ▶ a single parent who is not working
> ▶ divorced parents living separately with joint custody
> ▶ two parents, who are women in a lesbian relationship
> ▶ two parents, who are men in a homosexual relationship
> ▶ a step-parent and one biological parent
> ▶ foster parents

> ▶ a grandparent
> ▶ one or more parents with a disability
> ▶ parents with one, two or several children
> ▶ one parent from a minority ethnic group
> ▶ parents with different religions or cultures
> ▶ parents who have limited access to their children.

Nowadays relatively few children will be living in what was once regarded as a traditional family, with a mother at home, a dad at work and one or two siblings. Sometimes the media and government departments hark back to times when things were different. They make the assumption that everything was much better for children when parents conformed to this kind of stereotypical picture. As early years educators it is part of our job to challenge these kinds of stereotypes. We must appreciate the fact that children can thrive, be strong and happy and fulfilled with many different kinds of parents.

Nursery parents

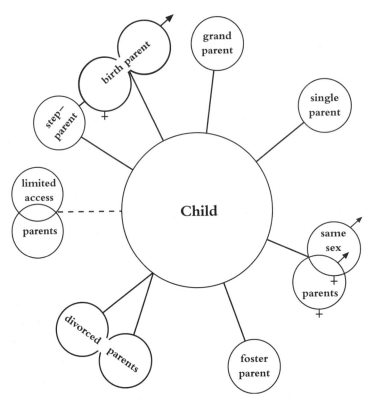

Examples of primary carers for children

Being a parent

Think about what the job of being a parent must be like for these parents.

> ▶ You are a harassed and hard-working single parent trying to balance your three year old child's needs with your own desire to get back to work or study and to have a small amount of personal space.
>
> ▶ You and your partner are bringing up a family of four and you have a two year old with special educational needs. You're struggling to communicate with a large number of professionals from the health, education and social services departments and at the same time you are trying desperately hard to meet the needs of the rest of your family.
>
> ▶ You have grown up as a 'client' of the system, either as a child in care or because at some point your own child was put on the child protection register or taken into care.
>
> ▶ Having grown up in a **majority world culture** you find yourself

isolated as a member of a minority ethnic group in a fairly hostile environment. You're trying hard to find a way into using services but your cultural needs don't appear to be recognised or celebrated.

▶ You and your partner both work. You travel a great distance and work long hours. You feel guilty because you want to spend more time with your children and you hardly ever spend time with your partner.

▶ You are an isolated father or mother living in poverty on income support with a two year old and a four year old.

▶ You have chosen to give up work to be at home with your children, but you feel lonely and isolated. Your partner doesn't understand what you do all day.

Parenting has been described as unpaid work which lasts a lifetime! It can be both incredibly rewarding, and emotionally and physically draining. Often as a parent you can go days, weeks or even months without any positive feedback from another adult on 'how you're doing'. It can be a very lonely job and parents are often very afraid that they're not getting it right. The parents in our examples have each taken on a job that involves them working 24 hours a day. Remember children are only in school for

SITUATION VACANT
WANTED: ONE MUM
ARE YOU –

- companion
- decorator
- counsellor
- cleaner
- taxi driver
- play supervisor
- nurse

- financial manager
- child care supervisor
- purchasing officer
- social secretary
- teacher
- diplomat
- cook

- willing to work long hours for low pay

Please apply to :
A family
10 The Street
Towby

Situation vacant?

approximately 16 per cent of their waking life. This means that these parents have to keep their children safe, well and support their development for the rest of the time. To do this they need to have a huge range of skills and expertise.

It's clear that parents have very little time left for themselves. It will be hard for them then to find time and energy to sign up for a course or attend a parent support group. Most parents when their children are very young are desperately grateful for even a small amount of 'time out' to:

– go to the loo without a little person hanging on to your jumper . . .
– relax on the sofa and read a book . . .
– go for a proper walk without having to stop a million and one times . . .
– just sit and think and do absolutely nothing . . .
– take time to be with their partner without having three other things to do
  at the same time.

As an early childhood educator it is important for you to think highly of the parents of the children in your care. You also need to feel good about working with them if you are to develop a genuine partnership. It may be that when you considered the list of different kinds of parents you found some of them hard to accept or understand. Your own parents may be very different from the parents of the children in your care.

Avoid being judgmental

If you had two parents yourself and your own experience of being parented was very positive, perhaps you feel that children in your nursery with one parent are automatically at a disadvantage?

Perhaps your parents worked long hours and you resented it. Now you think mothers ought to spend more time at home with their children. How do you feel about the working mums who drop their children off for breakfast in your nursery?

As an early years educator you should be careful not to be judgmental. If you find yourself thinking that certain kinds of combinations of parents are intrinsically better than others or if you feel uncomfortable or uneasy about certain kinds of parenting combinations then it is important for you to talk about your thoughts and feelings with your colleagues. In any staff group a diverse range of families will be represented. Some will have been brought up by single parents, others will have lived in traditional two-parent families. Some may have been brought up in care. You will find that some will have had happy childhoods but others may have been hurt or badly treated by their parents. Their positive and negative experiences of being parented will have had very little to do with the kinds of parents they had – gay, straight, divorced, married, step-parent or biological parents can all be effective parents. Their experience will have had much more to do with their parents' **style** of parenting.

Different parenting styles

Parents bring up their children in very different ways. Whilst there isn't one right way to be a parent, some parenting styles do seem to work better for children than others. In early childhood settings some of the ways that staff engage children and set boundaries with them are more effective than others and some just don't work at all!

There is a kind of rhythm in the way that parents 'work with' their children. After close observation of how parents settle their children in, play with them and separate from them, it can be said that parents' styles of being with and working with their children are characterised by:

> ▶ **anticipation** – parents seem to intuitively know what to do next when a child needs something physically or emotionally
>
> ▶ **recall** – the parents could share past experiences and relate them to what the children are doing or saying now while they play
>
> ▶ **mirroring experience through language** – parents can verbally reflect back to the children what they are doing
>
> ▶ **extending experiences and accompanying the child** – parents are quick to think about and show children new ways to approach things. They are also willing to follow their children's interest and give them the time and space to explore things
>
> ▶ **asking the child's view** – parents are interested in what their children are thinking and feeling
>
> ▶ **encouraging autonomy** – parents encourage their children to make choices and decisions
>
> ▶ **boundary setting/encouraging risk taking** – parents seem to know when to step in and how to encourage their children to have a go
>
> ▶ **judicious use of experience of failure/making mistakes** – parents support their children's right to experiment, to make mistakes and occasionally experience failure.

Not all parents are able to maintain these high standards all the time! Nor can it be expected that early years educators should maintain such standards of perfection.

Watching parents' positive parenting styles encourages staff to be more aware of how to work with children in the nursery. In a nursery, staff can build on the positive nurturing experiences that parents give to children at home. The structures and boundaries set by parents need to be maintained if children are to feel really comfortable and 'at home' in the nursery setting.

The following two case studies are examples of the different ways parents behave towards their children and their parenting styles give out strong messages to their children.

Three year old Sean has a single-parent father. When Sean comes into nursery and says 'My dad's proud of me', he shows that he feels both loved and lovable. He also knows that his father believes in his ability to do things. John, Sean's dad, takes him to dance once a week with 'the old folk', and on daily cycle rides. He takes Sean for walks through a public park which most nursery parents avoid since it tends to be a hangout for 'winos'. John's comment is that Sean knows all the winos by name! John is deeply committed to politics and talks of his son as a 'socialist soldier'. He is so concerned about his son's education that he attends a study group every week at the nursery where he can find out more about the early years curriculum and what his son is learning. John spends hours talking to Sean, listening to him, telling him stories and supporting his play. Clearly some children don't get such positive messages from their parents' parenting style, as Sean does. Some parents may be struggling too hard to be able to support their children appropriately. Perhaps their own experiences of being parented were very negative and damaging.

As an early childhood educator you will work with children like Sean who are having very positive experiences at home and you will also work with children like Christopher.

Christopher is three and a half and has been in and out of care three times already. Esther, his mum, was abused as a child and is now an alcoholic. Esther is a single parent, and every Thursday evening after she has received her benefit she goes out and gets drunk and is often incapable of looking after Christopher or his little sister. Christopher is very anxious when he comes into nursery and he needs lots of support from his special key worker. He generally holds his head down and makes little eye contact and is quiet and withdrawn. He often needs to be allowed to play in just one area of the nursery for long periods of time because he is frightened of anything new. Moving out of his safe play space is too daunting. He often wants the same story over and over again. Christopher needs a very predictable environment when he comes to nursery. He needs to be greeted every session by his key worker who makes sure he gets listened to in group times. Christopher's key worker home visits both Esther and his foster parents and this helps reaffirm the nursery's relationship with all the important adults in Christopher's life.

Clearly Sean's experience of being parented is more positive for him than Christopher's, although both have parents that love them very much. Sean and Christopher's parents both live on benefit and struggle to give their children the tangible things that more affluent children take for granted.

John and Sean spending time together

Both parents care deeply about what happens to their children and want them to have better experiences of the education system than they themselves had. Sean and Christopher are experiencing very different styles of parenting. Sean is getting a lot of **nurturing** from his dad, who loves and accepts him but also has high expectations of him. Sean has high self-esteem and is fairly confident. He is willing to have a go at most things at nursery. Sean's dad also provides him with a reasonable amount of **structure** in his life. John sets clear boundaries with Sean about what's okay and what is not okay.

Christopher, on the other hand, has a very chaotic and unstructured life. This means that nursery routines are incredibly important and useful to him. He doesn't ever know what will happen, for example, at the end of a week: will he end up in care or find himself in the middle of a row between his mum and the neighbours? Esther does nurture him a lot when she is feeling on top of things and Christopher knows that he is loved but he has very little confidence in his own abilities.

It isn't useful for us to judge parents like Esther and find them wanting. We need to recognise the pressures that work, unemployment, poor health and poverty all bring. Most parents want the best for their children. As an early childhood educator you may not share all the same values as the parents who use your nursery and you may not like some of the things that they are doing. However, it will be important for you to recognise and build on the positive aspects of their parenting styles.

Creating a dialogue with parents

. . . when we draw children, parents and families into our early childhood centres I think we should be sure that what we are about is making these people strong, providing them with the means to reshape their destinies, giving them a measure of control and influence about what goes on, encouraging them to stop accepting their lot and start creating the world they would like to be a part of (Chris Pascal, April 1996).

Working in partnership with parents can be painful and difficult for us as early childhood educators but it can also be enormously rewarding. Most parents are deeply committed to their children's learning and development. Also, parents have a critical role as their child's primary educator in the early years. Children are much happier and achieve more when early years educators work together with their parents.

Since parents are not a homogeneous group they all have different needs and different starting points. They will want to get involved in their children's early years settings in very different ways. They will need to make their own priorities, negotiate their own learning and do this in their own time.

Focusing on their children

Some parents may want to know more about their children's learning. Many of the parents who have worked with us at Pen Green over the last fourteen years have been very interested in their children's development. When parents are first offered a nursery place for their child they are encouraged to watch and record their child's persistent concerns at home. Many become fascinated by the repeated patterns they observe within their children's play. Some parents, supported by experienced staff, have kept diaries, others record what they see their children doing on audio tapes or using camcorders. Over the last few years parents have become very involved in a nursery-based research project. They have attended daytime and evening sessions to compare notes with nursery staff and watch video tapes of their children playing in nursery and at home. Together parents and staff have built up information about their children's learning which has supported our curriculum planning in the nursery. This way of working with parents is described in more detail in chapters 2 and 3.

Focusing on parents' own learning needs

For some parents getting their child a place in a nursery or day care centre is a very important first step in that it gives them the time and the space to consider their own learning needs. It may be that they are interested in attending a group on assertiveness, or massage and aromatherapy, or perhaps a short course on basic typing skills. They may want to develop their numeracy or literacy skills as a way to get back into work. Parents sometimes want to undertake GCSEs and A levels in a supportive environment or perhaps want to undertake longer-term Open University Community Education courses such as the new Confident Parents, Confident Children study pack. Other parents may want to attend groups that help and support them and keep them informed, such as a single parents' support group or a support group for parents with children who have special educational needs. In these groups parents get time and space to discuss their own concerns and their children's issues. Chapters 6, 8 and 10 give good examples of how to set up and run these kinds of groups in early years settings.

Focusing on other people

Parents may want to start their involvement careers in your setting by doing things that help your centre or by doing things for other people in the community. Having been at home for years doing things for their children and their families and friends they are most comfortable and confident in this role. Parents successfully run services such as playgroups, parent and toddler groups, toy libraries and nursery bookshops in many early years settings. It is important to offer parents training and support if they are running services of this kind. It will also be important sometimes to make a member of staff available from your own setting or from another agency to work alongside them. See chapter 7 for some good examples of this kind of shared work.

Parents can have a vital role on the management committee. Parent representatives are elected by other parents and represent their views and make policy alongside senior officers from funding agencies. In many early years settings parents now act as governors and managers. This is a very positive way for parents to express their own commitment both to the local community and to improving services for children and families.

Working in a holistic way

The most effective parenting programmes in early years settings combine at least some aspects of all three of these approaches.

1. **Action for children** – when the focus is on children and the parents are encouraged to watch their children, learn more about their children's learning process and perhaps work towards a qualification as an early years educator themselves.
2. **Action for parents** – when the focus is on parents' own learning and doing things for themselves. This could mean claiming their own right to an education second time around, or building up their own self-esteem.
3. **Action for others (citizenship)** – when the focus is on parents co-ordinating groups and activities that help other people, or when parents take responsibility for managing and running early years services.

In the past, professionals often assumed parents would start in one particular way, gain confidence and gradually get more involved in what was going on in a setting, following a kind of linear 'route'. This is only one way that parents can use parenting programmes. Figure 1.1 shows two possible routes through everything on offer at an early years centre. Many other parents, it is now recognised, want to access more than one kind of experience at the

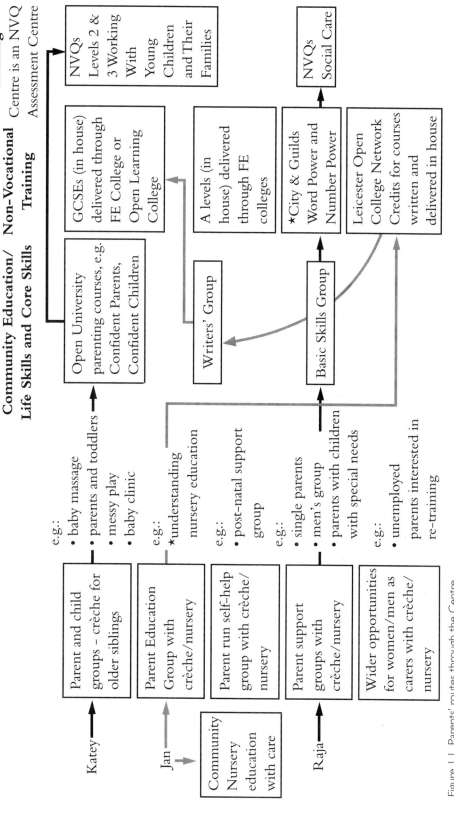

Figure 1.1 Parents' routes through the Centre

same time. Janet is a good example of a parent who uses early childhood settings in this kind of holistic way.

Janet was a single parent with four daughters under six years. When she started using the Centre she always kept her coat on, ready for a quick getaway. She always looked down when she talked to adults. Janet was very vulnerable: she had just moved into the estate and knew no-one.

Action for herself as a parent

During the first few months she began using a support group where she was able to talk about what was going on in her life to other women experiencing similar pressures. When she became pregnant she joined the Great Expectations group run by a parent and a midwife. (This group offers support to parents who have experienced stillbirth and/or miscarriage.)

Action for her children

Two of Janet's children were attending the nursery. Cath, her key worker, invited Janet to start sharing information about both her daughters' development and play at home. For a whole year, Janet kept audio tapes of her children's experiences at home. She identified the patterns in her daughters' play and shared her observations with the nursery staff. Particularly, she commented on her daughter Katey's preoccupation with putting things inside other things and playing with bags, baskets and boxes. The nursery staff were able to tell her that Katey loved putting herself inside things when she was in nursery, e.g. the toy washing machine, the tent, the parachute or enclosing herself with the building blocks. Janet decided to support her child's learning at Christmas by buying her a big pink bag instead of the usual gifts from toy shops. Katey loved the bag and filled it with objects both at home and at nursery.

Janet got very excited by and involved in her daughters' learning so she joined an informal parent education group to find out more about children's educational needs.

Janet made all the decisions about the level, nature and timing of her involvement in the adult community education programme. Most recently, after watching videos of her daughter in the nursery she and her partner made a video of their four daughters and new baby playing at home. This home video has informed the nursery staff's planning for children's learning.

Janet has taken herself seriously as a student. She has also gained confidence as a parent and recognises the major contribution she has made as her children's first educator.

Action for others

Janet holds her head upright when she talks to staff and other parents and expresses her views at Parents' Meetings. She also shares her understanding of Katey's learning with visitors from other nurseries.

Direct work with parents

Working so closely with parents puts enormous pressure on us as early childhood educators.

> ▶ We need to be able to involve parents and work with them as equal partners.
> ▶ We need to be able to share the decision-making with them and work in an empowering way.
> ▶ We need to be able to think about things from the parents' perspective.
> ▶ We need to believe in what we are doing.

Perhaps at this point you should take some time to talk to your work colleagues about your worst fears about sharing power with parents and encouraging them to feel at home in your setting. In a workshop made up of a large group of early childhood professionals these were the kinds of anxieties that people expressed.

My worst fear is . . .

> ▶ Parents will take over.
> ▶ They'll get into cliques and keep other parents out.
> ▶ We'll lose control of the nursery children.
> ▶ Having their parents in will confuse the children.
> ▶ Parents will want their own way all the time.
> ▶ We'll have problems with confidentiality.
> ▶ They'll eat us alive and want to take up all our time.

Talking out your worst fears, giving them a dusting down and then discussing them realistically with colleagues may be an important first step to becoming more actively involved in direct work with parents.

Summary

▶ There is a strong and radical tradition in the United Kingdom of working with parents as equal and active partners.
▶ Parents are their child's primary educators; children spend less than 16 per cent of their waking lives in schools. As early childhood educators we need to build on what they have learnt at home.
▶ Some parents may have had very negative experiences of schooling. They will find it hard to access parenting programmes in formal settings.
▶ As early childhood educators we have a lot to learn from parents about effective strategies for working with young children.
▶ Parents are not a homogeneous group; children thrive in a range of different family structures.
▶ Early childhood settings need to offer a range of services to parents. The kinds of provision offered must be based on a local diagnosis of what is needed. It is time that we listened to parents.

Bibliography

Athey, C., (1990) Extending Thought in Young Children. London: Paul Chapman Publishing.

Ball, C., (1994) Start Right Report; The Importance of Early Learning. London: Royal Society of Arts. London: DfEE and SCAA.

Bethlehem, B., (1987) A Good Enough Parent. London: Thames & Hudson.

Lowndes, G.A.N., (1960) Margaret McMillan: The Children's Champion. Museum Press.

Open University, (1996) Confident Parents, Confident Children: A Community Education Study Pack. Milton Keynes: Open University Press. This pack is a follow-up to the very successful Open University 'Pre-School Child' pack which was a bestseller.

Pascal, C., (April 1996) Higher Education Partnerships with Early Childhood Services. Pen Green lecture, unpublished.

Pascal, C. and Bertram, A. (eds), (1997) Effective Early Learning. London: Hodder & Stoughton.

Puckering, C., Rogers, J., Mills, M. and Cos, A.D., (1994) Mellow Mothering: Process & Evaluation of a group intervention. Mothers with Parenting Difficulties. Child Abuse Review 3, 299, 310.

Pugh, G., De'Ath, C. and Smith, C., (1994) Confident Parents, Confident Children, National Children's Bureau Publications.

Schools Curriculum and Assessment Authority, (1996) Desirable Outcomes for Children's Learning. London: DfEE and SCAA.

Smith, C., (1996) Developing Parenting Programmes. London: NCB Publications.

Stacy, M., (1991) Parents & Teachers Together. Milton Keynes: Open University Press.

Vincent, C., (1995) Schools Community & Ethnic Minority Parents. In Croft, M., and Tomlinson, S. (eds), Ethnic Relations & Schooling Policy & Practice in the 1990s. London: Athlone Press.

Whalley, M., (1994) Learning to be Strong. London: Hodder & Stoughton.

Useful contact

For further information on community education study packs write to:
Central Enquiry Service, PO Box 200, The Open University, Walton Hall, Milton Keynes, MK7 6YZ.

2

Shared Knowledge – Parents and Workers

In this chapter we consider the importance of understanding a child's situation or context. We examine the benefits that shared knowledge about the child and his or her family can bring to early years workers. We describe how to set up a warm and welcoming environment for parents and discuss the importance of the key worker system if we are to have positive relationships with parents as well as children.

> No other adult in the building can possibly know as much about this small new person as his parent does, and in the beginning the teacher (early years educator) must depend on the parent's knowledge in helping the child to settle happily in the nursery school (Department of Education for Northern Ireland, 1977).

Getting to know each other

Current research supports the belief that if we want to do the best for children we need to involve their parents and carers. It is now widely accepted that involving parents, listening to what they have to tell us about their child and accepting that they are their child's first educator will enrich the experience for the child in our care. Tina Bruce in the introduction to her book *Early Childhood Education* (1987) cites the need for us to become more 'child-in-the-family/community-centred' in our work with young children. In her later book *Time to Play* (1991), in which she develops the ideas around free-flow play, Bruce emphasises balancing the strands of the early childhood curriculum – the child, the content and the context.

> It would not make sense to try to educate a child without taking account of the most significant people in his/her environment (Bruce, 1987).

The child's context will include the people who are important influences, for example parents, extended family, childminders, as well as other factors such as the child's cultural background and race, gender, and possible special educational needs. It will also include the child's physical environment. Is the child within the family growing up in an isolated high-rise flat on a run-down inner-city estate and suffering from material disadvantage? Or does the child live in a comfortable rural setting with the support of extended family and friends? Is the child a black child living in a largely white community, or does the black child live within a multiracial community? All of these contextual factors will influence the child and his/her family. Let us look at a child, Jayne, and how having a shared knowledge about her and her context might influence us when we plan for her learning experiences within our setting.

Jayne is three years old and lives with her dad. She is an only child. Her dad, Paul, is on benefit. He does not see himself as having succeeded at school, and before the birth of Jayne he worked for the council as a care-taker at the local school. He has helped to set up a local youth club, because he cares very much about community facilities for children and young adults. He is a keen gardener, is interested in animals, wildlife and conservation. He does not own a car, and brings Jayne to nursery every day on the back of his bicycle. He is interested in politics and social justice and talks to her about these issues. They read a lot together at home.

Jayne's mum misuses alcohol and left the family home, at which point Paul fought through the courts to keep Jayne with him. Jayne sees her mother irregularly. She has access every Sunday, but Jayne is often disappointed when mum does not turn up for weeks on end.

Paul and Jayne live in a council house on a run-down housing estate. Paul and Jayne share long walks and bike rides in to the local countryside where they collect birds' feathers and leaves, and discover the skulls and bones of dead animals. Jayne brings these things into nursery to share with her carers.

How can all this sharing of knowledge about Jayne's context help us to extend these very rich experiences which Jayne is already enjoying at home? Or, to look at it another way, how could you, as an early childhood worker, begin to plan appropriate curriculum content for Jayne **without** all of this knowledge about her context? Once you know something of what is in her mind, then you as an adult can begin to understand what is important for her.

Tina Bruce is clear that our job, as early childhood educators, is to balance

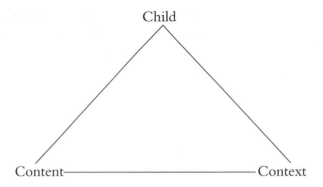

The 'Three Cs of Early Childhood Curriculum'

the three corners of the triangle of Early Childhood Education. She puts the child very firmly at the apex of the triangle, with the context and content as being equally important for the child's cognition and affective development.

She calls this the 'Three Cs of Early Childhood Curriculum' (Bruce, 1991).

You know Jayne is an only child and has had the undivided attention of a caring parent at home. Experiences which involve her within a small group of children, which demand turn-taking, sharing and negotiation might well be important.

You know that she often experiences a deep sense of disappointment at weekends when her mother does not turn up to visit her. Finding time to talk to her about her mum, showing your concern on Mondays when she comes into nursery, and acknowledging her feelings will be very important. You might take her on special outings with her friends or on a walk to the local park where she can extend her knowledge about wildlife. Allowing her the opportunity to share her knowledge with adults and other children about what she already knows, acknowledging that she is already an expert on feathers, will extend her sense of well-being and self-esteem. She may well already know more about her locality than you do, from her walks with her dad. Looking at maps of the local area together might lead to her being able to draw her own map of how to get from her house to the local park.

When she brings the skull of a dead bird which she has found when out on a walk with her dad, you will need to build on that interest. You might want to visit the local library and borrow books on birds and skeletons.

Only by knowing more of Jayne's context can you support what she already knows and also extend her into the unknown (what she has yet to learn). Initial findings from recent research by the New Zealand Council for Educational Research in the Competent Children Project (1995) suggest that involving parents in early childhood settings is not only of benefit to the child but also helps parents.

> **Parents told us that their involvement boosted their own skills and brought them support, friendship, enjoyment, a better understanding of their own child and a sense of achievement.**

Imagine how proud Jayne's dad must feel that the educators within his daughter's setting value what he is doing as a parent for his child. At a time when professional attitudes to parents and their contribution remain fairly negative and the media message is that 'parents don't care about their children', Paul is getting the message from his daughter's educators that they value him as a parent.

They also acknowledge what a good job he is doing, despite poverty and all the odds that are stacked against him.

The benefits

The immediate benefits to the child and his/her parents are that the child's experiences and self-esteem are enriched and the parents feel acknowledged and valued. How does all this extra work benefit you as the early childhood worker? If you are a playgroup worker earning £2.00 an hour, or a reception class teacher with 30 children in your class, you might want some reward for the extra time and effort you put into involving parents more in your setting.

Alison is a worker in a local authority provision for under-fives. She obtained her NNEB qualification at the local college. On her two-year course she received no training in involving parents (this might also be true for a lot of teachers). From college she went to work in a private work-place day nursery, attached to a factory. Because of her shift-working, and the fact that most parents dropped their children off in a rush to get to work, she rarely had time to find out about the children's context.

Now that she works in a setting which encourages parents to be involved in their children's learning she explains how she believes the quality of her work has been positively influenced by involving parents in their children's learning.

'I used to work in a private day nursery with two to five year olds, when the only brief contact I had with parents was when the child was dropped off and picked up. I was only allowed limited time to find out about the child's background, interests and enjoyments. I didn't have time, nor was I encouraged, to tell parents about what their child had been doing at nursery either. Because I'm not a parent myself, and I hadn't really been encouraged or taught how to talk to parents, I think I was a bit frightened to do it anyway, if I'm honest!

Now that I work here, and I've had the chance and the encouragement and extra training, I know a lot more about families. I know I'm much better at listening to parents, and I really do value the time I spend with them. It benefits the children, because I'm now better at settling the children and helping them enjoy nursery more. My job is much more varied and interesting. I wouldn't want to work any other way now.'

If you work in an early years setting, for example a playgroup, you may not have a budget for training. Perhaps you could contact your local Social Services Team Leader or U8s worker or the Child & Family Guidance Unit if there is one near you. They might be able to offer you some training or support, free of charge. If you want to think about changing the way you work, or to get fresh ideas on how to involve parents in your setting, read the chapter by Gillian Pugh on *Parental Involvement, Developing Networks between School, Home and Community* (Wolfendale (ed.), 1989).

Creating a welcoming environment

There is plenty of evidence that working alongside parents can benefit everyone – the child, the parents and the worker. An early years setting might be a relatively well-resourced local authority nursery or reception class, or it might be a playgroup run in a church hall, sports centre or community centre. Wherever it is you work you will want your setting to be friendly and welcoming to parents, carers, grandparents – all those important adults in children's lives. You will want your setting to reflect the multicultural society in which parents are living and children are growing up.

How does your physical environment appear to parents?

These are some questions to ask:

▶ Can parents get into the building with a pram or buggy?

▶ Do you have access for parents or children in a wheelchair?

▶ If a parent wants to come in to help, can the baby or younger sibling come too? It is worth checking if your public liability insurance covers you to have younger children on the premises. If not, or there are other reasons particular to your setting which make it unsuitable for younger toddlers or babies, maybe you could find creative ways to solve these difficulties. One school set up a rota of parents who were willing to help each other out with childcare.

▶ Does the entrance to the setting appear friendly? For example, are there photographs and images of dads and mums? Do the photos and images reflect a variety of differently constituted families – extended families, two-parent families, one-parent families, dad as the primary carer, mum as the primary carer?

▶ Is there somewhere where adults can sit on adult-sized comfortable chairs with newspapers, magazines and other reading material? If parents are feeling uncomfortable at the beginning, they may choose to hide behind a newspaper!

▶ Is there a welcome poster which features adults and children and is written in a variety of home languages? If the commercial ones are too expensive or don't suit your community setting, perhaps you could involve parents in making one which is relevant to your community's culture and reflects the languages spoken within your locality. The Equality Learning Centre has an excellent catalogue of resources, including inexpensive posters which feature positive images of children and families. You will find their address and telephone number at the end of this chapter.

▶ Do you have an area where it is safe for parents to have a hot drink? At Walkergate Nursery School in Newcastle, one teacher works in a mobile classroom. She believes it is very important to encourage parents to come in. Despite the small space in which she operates, she has created a parents' reception area, where a small group of parents can meet together and have a coffee and chat without mixing hot drinks and young children!

▶ Are toilets signposted, and are you able to designate one toilet as a men's room *and* baby changing area? Or is there an area where both mums and dads can change babies?

▶ Is there a parent noticeboard, telling parents what's available for them where they can browse, or put up their own notices?

▶ Do you have flexible settling-in times in the morning so that staff can have the opportunity to greet each parent and child individually? Perhaps at the moment you may have a set time to open the doors to all parents and children. Could you reorganise your staffing at this time to allow even one person to be available to individually greet parents and children? In one rural primary school the staff have one morning a week when 'formal' school doesn't start until 10.00 am. Parents know that they can come between 9 and 10 am on that morning to share information or raise any concerns. Children are also aware that at this time in the week the teacher or classroom assistant is 'busy' with dads and mums. It has become an established part of the school's weekly routine.

It is important to remember that parents coming to your setting may have only bad memories and feelings of failure about institutions. You may be able to do something about these feelings by making your setting more welcoming to parents and children. Whatever staffing or resourcing difficulties you face in your particular setting, parents will be appreciative of a friendly smile, a respectful greeting, and a cuddle for their child. You may not be able to change the circumstances of your setting, but you can change your attitude and methods of working and, by example, influence those of your colleagues.

Home visiting

One of the best ways of getting to know about a child's context is by visiting her/him at home. Home visiting has been regarded as the job of health visitors or Home Start volunteers, but has now become common practice for day nursery, family centre and reception class staff too. Home visiting has several key functions. It enables the worker to introduce him/herself to the parents/carers so that when they come to your early years setting they will see at least one familiar face. It is a chance for parents to find out something about you, and to ask you about the setting. Parents might feel more relaxed and enabled if they can do this on their own territory. Ideally the home visitor should be the person who will be caring for that child, their 'key worker'. (The role of the key worker is referred to later in this chapter.)

The primary purpose of the initial visit is to begin a warm, friendly relationship with the parents and child. It is best not to overwhelm parents on this visit by telling them everything there is to know about the setting. Choose some key points which you feel they need to know, such as:

> ▶ the settling-in period
> ▶ costs (if any)
> ▶ times of sessions.

You will want to listen to the parents and find out as much as you can about the child, for example:

> ▶ important adults in the child's life
> ▶ the child's and family's interests
> ▶ what the child likes to eat
> ▶ any health problems or food allergies
> ▶ what might help the child settle smoothly into the setting
> ▶ how the parents would like to handle the first moment of separation
> ▶ whether the child needs a sleep during the day (if he/she is attending full-time).

All of this information will become the basis for real communication with the child in the nursery, playgroup or reception class.

This may sound too frightening and unfamiliar to you if you have not had any suitable training in home visiting. Maybe one of your local health visitors could offer a training session, or you could carry out at least one home visit with a more experienced member of staff. If you think parents might be anxious as to why you would want to home visit, it would be best to make your reasons clear when you write to make an appointment with them.

It is important to include the following points in the letter.

> ▶ Staff from your setting visit all parents, not just those who are on the child protection register.
> ▶ The appointment time can be negotiated with the parent if the time you offer does not suit work shifts or family routines.
> ▶ An explanation of why you are coming should be made.
> ▶ You are sensitive and respectful of the family's cultural, religious and economic background.

Angela, an early years educator in a family centre, describes a home visit to a Muslim family.

As part of my role as a family worker I am expected to home visit children and families. On one particular visit to a Muslim family, I arrived just as the child's parents were about to start praying. Unfortunately I had not realised that I had arranged to visit at a time which was inconvenient for them. It was important that they prayed at a particular time that day as it was during Ramadan. I was treated with great respect. When I arrived a table had been laid with special celebration dishes, to be eaten after sunset. Zaki was at home with both of his parents, Sardi and Abid. They were very warm and friendly. Zaki's mother, Sardi, presented me with a bunch of yellow roses to symbolise our friendship.

Zaki's parents were very interested in his education both at home and at nursery. We shared the Centre's philosophy and discussed cultural differences at great length. Sardi waited on and served me food throughout the visit. I felt very honoured and extremely special. Zaki's father Abid invited me to stay for dinner as a way of thanking me for the time I had spent with them as a family and for having his only son in my family group at nursery. I had not expected to be treated in this way and was flattered that I was seen as such an important person, as a teacher, in their culture.

Finding time to home visit will be particular to your individual workplace. If you work in an infant school with a non-teaching head, you may be able to negotiate that the head takes your class for the last hour in every day over a period of weeks to release you to home visit. If you work in a nursery class or unit you may be able to stagger the intake so that you can get out on home visits. If you believe home visiting is central to the way you work, you will need to think creatively about how you can make it happen.

Settling in to nursery

Having begun a sharing relationship on the first home visit, how can you now develop this? One way might be to establish a 'settling-in period'. This would involve the child being accompanied, say for the first two weeks, by an adult who is important in the child's life. This familiar adult could be a parent, childminder, grandparent or other adult member of the family, or even a neighbour. If you establish this as one of your good practice principles and it is discussed fully with parents, then you are unlikely to have any complaints. You can make it easier for parents if you encourage them to negotiate this settling-in time around their annual leave from work and you can be flexible about starting dates. Parents will be just as keen as you for their child to settle well. If you stress the long-term benefits of a well-settled child, parents will only be too happy to co-operate. This settling-in period may put extra demands on both you and the parent. You might both have concerns.

PARENTS' CONCERNS	EARLY YEARS WORKERS' CONCERNS
▶ I'll be embarrassed if my child won't play with others and clings to my leg.	▶ What will I do if the child keeps going back to their parent?
▶ What will I do if my child has a tantrum or hits another child?	▶ What if the parent doesn't like my style of being with their child?
▶ What if my child won't share with others?	▶ What if my group time, when I want children to sit down, is a shambles?
▶ What if I cry when I need to leave?	▶ What if there is conflict between the parent and child?

If we, as early years workers, can be humble enough to ask parents to share their expertise about their child we can learn a lot from them about their child's individual needs. For instance, the parent can tell us how the child likes to be comforted when he/she is upset. What successful strategies does the parent use? If the child is unwilling to sit down for a story it would be important to ask the parent what he/she might enjoy at group time. Remember that the parent is an expert and has valuable help to give. You can use these times as opportunities to learn. This will benefit your long-term relationship with the child. If parents can see staff making mistakes, or not getting it quite right, then it may be easier for them to relax when their child is difficult.

A key worker system

A key worker system is already common practice within a social work model. A social worker will have a case load of families and be the person with special responsibility for the needs of particular clients or families. Generally the social worker takes full responsibility for these families and receives supervision and support from a more senior member of the social work team. This is a model you may wish to integrate into your practice, in part or full.

There is good evidence that secure attachments in nursery are critical to children's healthy emotional and cognitive development. Peter Elfer describes intimate relationships as 'close, sensitive, responsive and respectful' (Sheffield Seminar Series, April 1995). He cites various examples of research which suggest that these close relationships are vital to a young child's affective development, whilst he remains doubtful if such relationships are present in practice. The integration of a key worker system is an opportunity to ensure that our relationships are 'close, sensitive, responsive and respectful'.

The system in practice

The basis of a key worker system is that each child and family is assigned to an individual worker within the setting. This in itself would not ensure intimacy – for that, some other tasks would be important:

> ▶ to carry out a home visit
> ▶ to greet the child each day on arrival and facilitate an easy separation from the child's primary care giver

Marcus, a family worker, settling Harry into nursery

> ▶ to observe the child's play, interact with and support the play and plan to extend his/her learning
> ▶ spend planned time with the child on an individual or small group basis each day.

Of course each child will have to share their key worker with other children and they will probably be cared for by other members of staff throughout the day as well. If a child falls over during outside play the member of staff 'anchored' in that area will initially deal with the child's distress. But it will be the key worker's responsibility to tell the parents at the end of the session/day about the circumstances of the fall and what action was taken.

Some early years settings are more hierarchical than others. In some, the head or supervisor may want to retain some overall responsibilities for children and families. In others, the head or supervisor might be happy to devolve responsibilities and act only in a supportive and supervisory role. In some settings the key worker will be responsible for attending, for example, case conferences to represent the child/family and the setting. In others the head or supervisor might wish to retain this role, or attend alongside the key worker. If you are new to this idea of a key worker system you might want to assume responsibilities gradually until you feel more confident. The amount of responsibility you assume as a key worker might be dependent upon your setting's staffing ratios. If you work on a 1:13 staffing ratio it may be more difficult for you to be released to attend meetings outside your setting.

Benefits and difficulties

As already mentioned, the primary benefit to the child is a strong emotional attachment to one key member of staff. But the key worker system will benefit parents and carers too.

> ▶ Parents may find it easier to share more intimate information or to ask for advice if they are finding some aspect of their parenting difficult.
>
> ▶ Each parent will get an individual greeting and be offered the opportunity to pass on any important information about their child, for instance if the child has had breakfast or slept well. Or they may want to tell you about a recent significant event for the child, for example, an outing, or the arrival of a pet. This information can be used by you to further your intimate relationship with the child.

As an early years educator and key worker, you can build on your skills and knowledge base.

> ▶ If you have a child within your group who has a special educational need, perhaps you will have the opportunity to learn about the child statementing process and be that family's 'named person' (see chapter 8).
>
> ▶ You will be able to offer continuity of care as younger siblings come into nursery or playgroup – you are already a trusted person whom the younger child in the family will know through daily contact and regular home visiting.

What might be the drawbacks?

> ▶ *What if I have a clash of personality with a particular child or parent?* Hopefully you will have established an open and honest relationship where you will be able to discuss any difficult issues which may arise. If you have a flexible provision children will be choosing their friendships with adults as well as with other children. You may have to accept that a child does prefer to be in someone else's group. This is unlikely to arise however, if you have done your 'homework' on the home visit and you are doing everything you can to meet each child's individual needs in your setting.
>
> ▶ *What happens if I'm ill or on holiday?* You will need to think about making provision for these situations in advance. If you know you are going on holiday or away for training, ask parents and children who they would like as their temporary key worker. If a 'supply' member of staff is to be used, try to introduce them before the event.
>
> ▶ *What if a child in my group doesn't want to come to playgroup/ nursery?* No matter how well a child appears to have settled in there may be a time when he/she becomes unsettled and unsure. It would be easy to take this personally. Talk it through with parents. It might be important to do an extra home visit to reassure the child and re-establish your closeness. Talk about it with the child, be honest and respect his/her fears. There may be a specific worry, for example 'Mummy might not come back', 'My friend says she doesn't want to play with me'.

Feedback from parents

It is important to constantly review what is being offered to parents and children. If you regard what you are offering as a service, paid for through fees or through local taxation (if you are part of a statutory service) then you need to offer value for money. One way of reviewing the service is by asking parents what they think. Each meeting with a new family will give you an insight into providing quality for parents and children. There are as many ways and styles of bringing up children as there are families. You need to be inventive in finding new ways and opportunities for families to express what they value about nursery or playgroup and also to tell you how they would want it to change or develop. Society, and with it family patterns and structures, changes all the time. If women in the community tend to return to work, is a two-hour playgroup session still going to be useful? If parents tell us that they find the parenting of two year olds the most stressful, and we continue to offer our services exclusively to three and four year olds, are we being responsive to parents' needs?

Are you able to change the service you offer, or offer an additional service? If you can find ways within your setting to give parents the opportunity to help make those changes it will not only be empowering for parents, it can also feel liberating for you.

In one early years setting where staff felt they could not find time to home visit, and new parents said they would like to be home visited, one parent came up with a good idea. His suggestion was that more established parents could do an initial visit to tell them about the service. This is now a successful part of introducing new parents to the setting.

In a playgroup the practice was to make all parents wait at the beginning of the session and be admitted as a group. Parents were able to say how unhelpful and distressing it was for their child to have to say a hasty goodbye. Now that staff have introduced a more informal and relaxed start, they can see the benefits for themselves, the children and the parents. Parents in a group might want time to meet together with their key worker to discuss issues particular to the interests of that group, for example practical issues such as how home and nursery can tackle toilet training together. If you do decide to have regular parents' meetings you will need to consider issues such as:

> ▶ time of day, to suit the majority of parents
> ▶ providing minutes for those parents unable to attend
> ▶ who will take the minutes
> ▶ running a crèche for siblings
> ▶ making the meeting as informal and friendly as possible
> ▶ setting the agenda. If parents are involved, then their issues must be included
> ▶ giving advance notice of the meeting. Parents may have to make special arrangements to be there
> ▶ who will chair the meeting.

It may be that your setting does not currently allow you the time, staffing and resources to run meetings in the evening with a crèche. You could however try working towards having a more flexible start to the session, when parents will feel able to have a friendly chat about their child.

Figure 2.1 on page 40 suggests a mixture of several ways that one family centre has devised (over many years) of giving and receiving feedback:

> ▶ three home visits a year including the initial visit before the child starts
> ▶ daily chats

A settling-in booklet

▶ a settling-in period (this setting negotiated a two-week settling-in period)

▶ a short booklet, which is given to parents after the two-week settling-in period, telling them what their child has enjoyed and if any difficulties have arisen. This booklet might be especially useful for working parents who only have contact with you through a childminder or other carer

▶ any training that staff receive which might be shared with parents

▶ a monthly evening meeting (in this example it's called the Centre Forum) where parents are invited to contribute to the agenda. The meeting could be chaired by a parent

▶ any workshops or groups you might run for parents, or they might run for you! You may have parents in your setting with particular skills, for example computers, cookery, gardening. Parents could teach staff new skills to enhance the curriculum you offer.

Any of these suggestions might help you to achieve the 'desirable outcomes' outlined by the School Curriculum and Assessment Authority (1996). The following points are made in relation to parents as partners in their children's learning:

- children's experiences at home are highly significant to achievement
- parents significantly influence their children's learning
- when parents and adults in each setting work together to support children's learning, the results can have a measurable and lasting effect upon children's achievement.

Record keeping

If you wish this dialogue to continue on an ongoing basis you might also consider asking parents to contribute to record keeping, as many nurseries do. If you consider a child's record as a kind of portfolio to which parents, staff and children can all contribute, you can build a comprehensive record of the learning which is happening both at home and school. Since young children spend more than 75 per cent of their time at home we would be ill-advised to ignore the enormous wealth of knowledge that the parents can contribute from home. Parents and children can bring in photos from home, to which staff can add photographs and drawings from nursery.

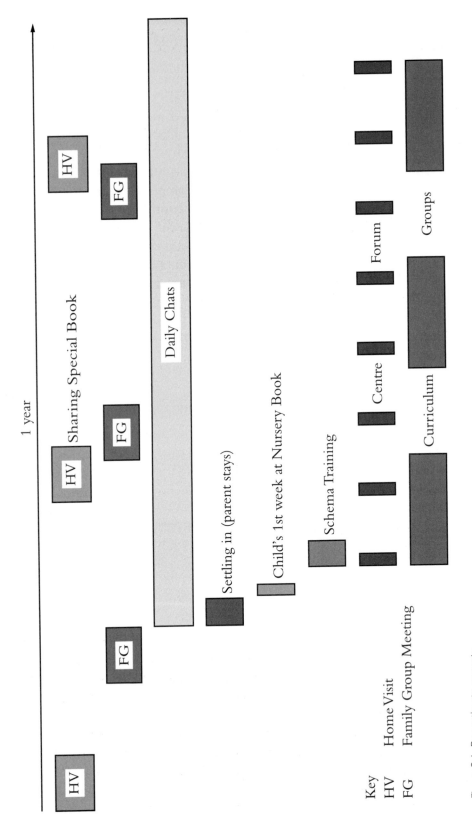

1 year

HV

Sharing Special Book

FG

HV

FG

Daily Chats

Settling in (parent stays)

Child's 1st week at Nursery Book

Schema Training

Curriculum

Centre

Forum

Groups

FG

HV

Key
HV   Home Visit
FG   Family Group Meeting

Figure 2.1 Reporting to parents

Parents can continue to add any new information about their children's learning which they consider important – about domestic and family events, or outings. This record can then be used as a focus for discussion on any future home visits or at nursery meetings. This record will become the property of the family when the child leaves the setting to move into the next stage of his/her schooling. It will be a treasured lifetime memento for each parent and child. See chapter 3 for further discussion on record keeping.

Identifying your training needs

Some settings will have training budgets. If so, it will be important to invite parents to train alongside staff. The Pre-School Learning Alliance organises training for playgroup staff, and actively supports parents through training to become playgroup staff. Many social services departments employ under 8s advisers who may help and advise about training opportunities which parents and staff can undertake.

Working with parents is now a key element in NVQ training and in several of the new early years courses. For example the BA Early Childhood Studies Course at the University of North London has a whole module written around working with parents. This course can be undertaken on a distance learning basis. If your initial training has not included any material on working with parents it is important for you to try to gain a real understanding of the issues. If your setting has no training budget then it may be possible for you to approach your local early years forum and ask them to set up an appropriate course.

Summary

> ▶ Parents want to be involved in their children's learning at nursery as well as at home and there are ways in which we can facilitate this – the very simplest being to have the right attitude and a determination to find a way.
> ▶ Parents' involvement in their children's learning has positive outcomes for staff (increased job satisfaction), parents (self-esteem, empowerment and assertiveness) and children (enhanced self-esteem, well-being and learning).

Bibliography

Bruce, T., (1987) Early Childhood Education. London: Hodder & Stoughton.

Bruce, T., (1991) Time to Play in Early Childhood Education. London: Hodder & Stoughton.

Schools Curriculum and Assessment Authority, (1996) Desirable Outcomes for Children's Learning. DfEE and SCAA.

Elfer, P., (1995) Sheffield Seminar Series: Facilitating Intimacy Between Adults and Young Children. London: National Children's Bureau.

Meade, A. with Cubey, P., (1995) Thinking Children, Competent Children Project, New Zealand Council for Educational Research and Institute for Early Childhood Studies, Wellington College of Education.

Department for Education for N. Ireland, (1977) Theory into Practice in a Nursery School. London: HMSO.

Wolfendale, S. (ed.) (1989) Parental Involvement, Developing Networks between School, House and Community. London: Cassell.

Wylie, C., (1996) Five Years Old and Competent. New Zealand Council for Educational Research.

Useful contacts

Equality Learning Centre, 356 Holloway Road, London N7 6PA (0171 700 8127).

New Zealand Council for Educational Research, Distribution Series, PO Box 3237, Wellington, New Zealand (fax from the UK 0064 4 384 7933).

Early Childhood Studies Scheme, Distance Learning Programme, University of North London, 116–220 Holloway Road, London N7 8DB.

3

Sharing Ideas with Parents about How Children Learn

> Nothing gets under a parent's skin more quickly and more permanently than the illumination of his or her own child's behaviour (Athey, 1990).

This chapter explores **why** it is a good idea for parents and early years workers to share ideas about how young children learn, and **how** parents and workers can share knowledge about young children learning. It identifies **what** knowledge it is helpful to share, **when** there are opportunities to share information and concludes by looking at **who** benefits from sharing ideas about learning.

Why share ideas?

When children start nursery, whether they are two, three or four years old, they are already very knowledgeable and skilled in many areas. Human beings learn all the time but the early years is a particularly sensitive period.

Acknowledging what young children know and can do

Children have already developed some complex ideas about their world when they begin nursery. They have knowledge about people, events, routines and rules within their own families, as well as knowledge of the physical environment that they have had opportunities to explore. Children usually know where they are allowed to play, what they can do there and often understand why different rules apply. For example, three year old Karl knows he is only allowed to play in the back garden, though his sister Katey can play on the pavement at the front of their house.

Young children are very skilled. In under two years, most have learned to sit up, crawl, walk and jump, as well as a host of other physical movements. Many children can already feed themselves. Often they are using a wide vocabulary of expressive language or sounds. Some children already speak more than one language.

Two-way communication is part of their repertoire and, by the age of two, they play games, such as 'peepo', 'round and round the garden' and 'row the boat', co-operating with familiar adults and children.

Young children are certainly not 'empty vessels' waiting to be filled with knowledge transmitted by adults.

Parents know their own children best

The people who have passed on this huge amount of knowledge and taught their children all these skills are usually each child's parents or main carers.

The important adults in the child's life:

> ▶ are alongside their child, often day and night
> ▶ have introduced their child to language through familiar songs and rhymes
> ▶ lovingly pass on their values and attitudes
> ▶ have encouraged their child to explore, to be independent, to care for others and to learn new skills
> ▶ have experienced and know how to react to their child's anger, sadness or joy.

Often parents worry about their children and how they will fit into nursery. Nursery workers, with their knowledge of child development, will need to reassure parents that each child is unique and valued equally. For example, some children aged two are potty trained while others are not ready to use a potty or toilet for another year or more. Workers can draw on their experience of other children to reassure parents that this is normal. Parents sometimes worry that their child will not be able to ask a member of the nursery staff for what he/she needs. They are also concerned that the nursery staff will be too busy to listen to their child. Again, it is important for you as an early childhood educator to acknowledge this as a real concern and to put the parent's mind at ease.

CHILDREN AS UNIQUE INDIVIDUALS

Each child has a unique set of experiences which no other human being has experienced in exactly the same way.

Children react in different ways. If you watch two children arriving at nursery you will see an example of this. One may sidle in clinging to their parent and need ten minutes of settling and reassuring, while the other may dash in ahead of an adult and immediately become involved in hammering nails at the woodwork bench, hardly noticing the parent leave.

Although aspects of development are shared by young children, mostly there are differences in the nature and speed of progress. A child may learn to walk at any time from eight months to almost two years within the normal range. Similarly, one child of eighteen months speaks clearly, while another three year old child uses only a few words.

Children (unless from multiple births) generally look different physically. Each child has a unique appearance. When workers treat children as unique individuals, they convey the message that we are all different and special.

As an early years worker, you need to be interested in finding out what is different about each child in your care. The account taken of those different motives, interests, actions and concerns means that you value each child's contribution to the nursery community and to your shared relationship.

Children who are different because of having special educational needs have not always been educated alongside other children of the same age. You need to recognise that we all learn from everyone we meet and spend time with. Greater differences between people mean greater learning for everyone involved. James' story gives a good example of this.

When James, a blind child, joined our nursery, staff had to think very carefully about how he could experience everything that was available to the other children. None of the children could tell the time but other children saw workers beginning to tidy up and prepare for storytime. The other children could see where each group met and who was there. All of the children in James' group benefited when the routine was adapted and included the lighting of a scented candle to signify the start of storytime. Each child in the group would introduce him/herself by name and greet each other by shaking hands or patting shoulders. There was a reason to speak and listen to each person in turn and if anyone was missing, we would talk about why he/she was not at nursery or at our group that day. It was important to ask James' parents what his interests and favourite stories were, so that we could build in that information. His parents naturally knew what he wanted to learn about.

Parents and workers can both be involved in finding out new information about a child's interests and concerns, and usually both can contribute valuable and different information.

Getting parents involved

Most parents are keen to share knowledge of their own children if opportunities are created for them to do so. It is important for workers to be open to and value parents' views. Workers can offer information and reassurance to the parents about what their children do when they are not around.

Listening and talking

The most natural means of communication for parents and early years workers to use is talking and listening. A dialogue can begin with the first home visit and should continue on a daily basis. Often, parents or carers bring young children to nursery and collect them. Part of the greeting between the worker and the child and parent might be a genuine enquiry about what the child has been doing. There is no formula to follow, except to have a joint interest in the child's well-being and progress.

As an early childhood educator you can use strategies to encourage this daily sharing. For example, by writing things down you are showing parents that you value the information they have given you.

If the child is not brought to nursery by a parent or if the parent is always in a desperate hurry because of work or because of taking other children to school, then there are other ways of carrying out an ongoing dialogue. A home/nursery book could be started. This would travel back and forth and contain short, written messages from parent to worker and back again. The child could contribute to this book and would learn a great deal about the written word and communication. (This method is often used by staff in special schools, when children are referred to a nursery by Social Services or other agencies, or are transported to nursery by escort drivers.)

Not all parents may be confident enough to share their writing. Audio tapes can be sent back and forth in the same way to convey messages. Favourite songs or stories can be recorded as part of this communication.

Storybooks can be loaned to children. These might help children in their transition to nursery, providing something special and chosen by the child to take home and to bring back on the following day. This custom also enables parents to familiarise themselves with their child's favourite stories.

Parents can loan storybooks to nursery. This is essential if the child has a second or third language, or is part of a minority ethnic group with which the worker is less familiar.

Special opportunities for discussing children's progress need to happen throughout the year. Visits to a child and family at home create a unique opportunity for parents to talk on their home ground. It may seem too public in the nursery to discuss worries or to check on a child's progress.

Meetings can be arranged as often as is practicable, when the parents can set the agenda. For example, a parent might want to complain about bullying or ask why their child comes home with paint on his/her clothes.

Parents can be invited in to discuss the curriculum.

Parents can be invited to take part in trips and special events.

Remember that if parents are to be given an equal opportunity to attend meetings, then they should be asked when is the most convenient time and day. If as an early years educator you really want to give every parent a chance to attend, then it may be necessary for some staff and parents to care for the children and siblings in an adjoining room. It could be a split meeting using a sort of 'shift' system, i.e. half of the people attend the meeting and the other half care for the children, then they swap over.

Sharing photographs

One very vivid and immediate way of sharing knowledge with parents about their children is to use photographs. Again, this can be a two-way communication tool.

Often young children enjoy bringing photographs of themselves and their families to show other children and adults at nursery. These may be of a holiday, a celebration or of a family event. This helps children and their parents to introduce a little of what happens at their home to the important people in the child's life at nursery. Photographs helped Chloë to settle at nursery.

Chloë started nursery at two and a half years old. Shortly afterwards her mother started work and her father took on the full-time care of Chloë and her brother. Around this time, she became a little unsure and unsettled. On a home visit, the parents and worker discussed what might help her to feel more 'at home' at nursery. Her mother was showing the family album and Chloë was talking nineteen to the dozen about herself and her family. Her parents loaned a set of photos to the worker, who had them copied. She then made a book with Chloë using the photos and Chloë's own language as a script. This enabled Chloë to talk about her worries, as well as sharing a little bit of her home with friends at nursery and, in doing so, she became an author for the first time.

Photographs are a useful record of what a child has been involved in at nursery. They can show what a child has been doing and who they have been with. Several photographs can be taken over a few seconds or minutes to illustrate what happens during a period of play. A single snapshot, unless accompanied by language, offers less information.

Photographs, whether a snapshot or a sequence, do provide something specific as a focus for discussion. Sometimes a parent will reveal information when looking at photographs taken at nursery. A worker may be puzzled by a child's actions or by a new friendship he/she has made. The parent can often offer possible explanations or figure out why. For example, Johnny was photographed while stacking crates and saying he was 'doing the dancing'. His parents understood exactly what he meant and explained that he went along to Scottish dancing each week with his older sister – he was using the crates to construct a stage for the 'dancing'.

Photographs are an expensive resource, but they can be used instead of costly display materials and are really valued by parents and children. Sometimes it may be necessary to ask parents to contribute to the cost. In that case, it would be important to give the photographs to the family after they have been displayed in nursery.

Another way of reproducing images of children is to capture video sequences on a computer and print out the chosen images and sequences. Although the initial cost is high, this method is a lot cheaper than photography. The images are not as sharp but the quality is reasonable.

Displaying a series of photographs illustrates the learning process more effectively

Sharing video material

Often parents express their wish to be a 'fly on the wall', to see what their child does and says when they are not around. A video camera enables early years workers to fulfil this wish for parents. The video camera is a unique tool in the sense that it can replay original words and actions over and over again. The film can also serve as a permanent record of a child's progress, a trip out or special event. Many families have camcorders and, again, video can form part of a two-way communication between the family and the people at nursery. Parents who film their children at home and share the footage with workers, give the workers an insight into the 'real' child at home.

Making sense of children's actions

Both parents and early years workers interpret what young children do in many different ways. Sometimes parents interpret children's actions in the light of family history, by comparing siblings or by recognising themselves as children in their own children's behaviour.

Parents are very good at making connections between what young children do at nursery and what the children have seen or experienced at home.

Early years workers can share other more general theories of child development with parents. Over the years, parents and early years educators have collaborated to observe young children at play in order to make sense of the children's actions (Arnold, 1990 and 1991; Athey, 1990; Gura, 1992; Meade and Cubey, 1995; Nutbrown, 1994; Rice, 1996; Whalley et al, 1997). Both parents and workers seem intrigued by what is going on inside each child's head as they learn.

When carrying out a recent project on 'Parents' Involvement in their Children's Learning', staff at Pen Green decided to share **two theories** of child development to help parents make sense of their children's actions (Whalley et al, 1997). The first theory helps to link patterns of action with knowledge gained by identifying children's **schemas** (behavioural patterns). The second enables us to recognise 'deep level learning' within each child by observing the child's **level of involvement**.

Theory 1: Using schemas to interpret actions

Parents and early years workers often used to have the notion that young children were unable to concentrate. Often children were described as 'flitting' from one activity to another. Recent research has indicated that young children are often 'fitting' pieces of information together in a systematic exploration of their environment (Athey, 1990).

Piaget called these patterns of action, used by children when fitting pieces of information together, 'schemas'. His work has been developed in recent years by practitioners in the UK and in New Zealand.

Recognising schemas is helpful to parents and early years workers in many ways. Schemas are patterns but they do not seem to appear in a set order. There is no set hierarchy and therefore no contest to reach, pass or complete. Each child shows different patterns although similarities are recognisable. Some children display one schema more dominantly. Others display a cluster of schemas.

Knowing about schemas enables us to understand some of the odd things children do, for example, unravelling a toilet roll instead of simply using the toilet paper or being more interested in the wrapping paper than the gift. Understanding about schemas helps both parents and staff to 'nourish' them and to offer each child provision based on knowledge of her current 'cognitive concerns'. We need to recognise and respect the fact that the young children in our settings often have a deep interest in a particular concern. They need time to explore their interest fully. When their interests or cognitive concerns are supported by early childhood educators, children learn at a much deeper level.

Some of the many early patterns recognised by parents and early years workers are described below:

A child who is interested in vertical trajectories or up and down movements might:

> ▶ jump up and down
> ▶ be fascinated with running water
> ▶ like building high
> ▶ and enjoy carrying sticks.

A child who is interested in horizontal trajectories or side to side movements might:

> ▶ place objects in a line or row
> ▶ enjoy pushing prams or trolleys
> ▶ constantly walk on lines
> ▶ like sweeping or mopping the floor.

Children fascinated by transporting objects or themselves from place to place might:

> ▶ carry bags containing various objects
> ▶ push prams or trolleys with objects or people inside them
> ▶ carry water from sink to bath
> ▶ enjoy playing picnics.

A child investigating rotation might:

> ▶ enjoy using whisks
> ▶ like turning a globe
> ▶ love sitting on a swivel chair
> ▶ frequently watch the washing machine or drier.

A child trying out patterns of behaviour is building up an increasingly complex picture of his/her world and of how things work within it.

Research is beginning to show where each schema may be leading.

> ▶ A child who is lining up identical objects is carrying out early measurement.
> ▶ A child who is transporting objects is learning about the conservation of number.
> ▶ A child who is representing enclosures in his drawing is learning how to form some letters of the alphabet.
> ▶ A child who is rotating his body is learning how to perform a pirouette.

When children are trying out their schemas on objects in their environment, at nursery or at home, and are supported in this by adults with language to match their actions and permission to try out their ideas, their motivation is high. If children feel unsupported or are constantly stopped from doing what they want to do, then they become frustrated and do not achieve their potential. For example, staff at one nursery, who knew nothing about a transporting schema, were puzzled when Kara kept trying to push a pram containing dough to the home corner. Her interest was not in the pram but in transporting. If the staff had known about schemas, they could have offered her other materials to transport varying in weight and size. They could also have suggested she use other modes of transport. This would have really extended her knowledge and understanding.

If children are involved in investigating their burning interest, they may be displaying patterns of action or schemas and they are **also** likely to be involved in 'deep level learning' (Laevers, 1993).

Theory 2: Recognising 'deep level learning'

Parents know a great deal about their own children and are acute observers but, like many early years workers, are not always sure what to write down, film or photograph, when keeping a record of their child's actions.

The Leuven Involvement Scale for Young Children helps to pinpoint when to record. Laevers (a researcher from the University of Leuven) developed the concept of an involvement scale. He believed that early childhood educators could judge how involved a child was in any learning situation by watching closely and picking up on body language and signals (Laevers, 1994).

The signs to look out for are:

> ▶ concentration
> ▶ energy
> ▶ complexity and creativity
> ▶ expression and posture
> ▶ persistence
> ▶ accuracy
> ▶ reaction time
> ▶ language
> ▶ satisfaction.

Involvement can be judged on a scale from high to medium or low involvement. If a child is enthusiastic, he/she has eyes that are bright, moves quickly to carry out his/her own ideas, shows determination and is not easily distracted, then the chances are that involvement in what he/she is doing is very high.

The idea of involvement is fairly easy to grasp and can be used to discuss the provision being made for individual children. A child's involvement would not rate as high the whole of the time at nursery or at home, but if it was constantly low you would know that you were not providing appropriate materials or supporting the child's interests. One key feature of high involvement is that you cannot distract a child who is highly involved. So if a parent or worker gets out the camcorder and the child is more interested in the camera than in anything else, he/she was not highly involved!

Parents and workers can all learn to recognise involvement, but you may not always have the energy to act on the information you have. One dad describing his daughter playing at home said, 'She was highly involved then it dipped to low, but she was driving me mad – I knew I could help but I'd had enough!'

Recognising the involvement signals and judging whether involvement is high or low, focuses the adults directly on the child. The scale is not used to judge the child or his/her ability, but it simply helps early years educators and parents to understand how closely they are meeting the child's needs at any moment in time.

The Leuven Involvement Scale in practice

You can offer your ideas to parents and listen to theirs. Discussing the involvement scale and 'having a go' at watching out for when a child is highly involved or when he/she is uninvolved is helpful. You may not always agree but in discussing your differing views you will gain a clearer understanding of the child and his/her interests and rhythms. Each child has a natural rhythm. One parent was worried that her child flopped down on the settee every afternoon and watched videos, and seemed uninvolved in exploration at home. The same child used up a great deal of energy at nursery each morning, dressing up, getting into various roles, negotiating with other children and adults, organising the home corner, and listening to and telling stories among other things! It is not surprising that she wanted to relax for a while after all that activity.

The involvement scale is a useful tool, but it is important to:

> ▶ try it out with colleagues and parents and establish some consistency about what you see as high or low levels of involvement (short video clips can be watched and discussed in staff meetings or at parents' evenings)
> ▶ practise using it – it may help you to see the nursery and what is happening there in a new way
> ▶ share as much as you know with the parents of the children you

are observing – whether they are working directly with you or not, parents have a right to know what is currently happening in their child's nursery

▶ see involvement as giving you some new knowledge about young children and learning.

Sharing theories with parents and colleagues

Sometimes it can seem daunting to share everything you know with others, particularly when you have just come across a new idea. If you are newly trained you may feel that everyone else working in the nursery is much more of an expert than you. They may be better informed, but they became well informed by trying out ideas, sharing, discussing, defending their principles, reading, watching young children and coming to new understandings as a result of their observations and discussions.

Sharing theories can be viewed as a means of discovering their usefulness in the real, everyday world of education. This means that as an early years worker you are on the front line – an explorer searching for new knowledge based on your own and others' practice.

Lynsey started nursery at two years one month. She was the youngest of four children who were all very close in age. She was very small and would point and grunt when she wanted something. Despite her size and age, she was very determined and had a clear ability to be deeply involved in whatever she chose to play with at nursery. She could concentrate for long periods and carried out her own explorations in a systematic way. Her schemas were easily identified and one piece of play was soon recorded in a sequence of photographs (shown on page 56).

Her parents realised that she liked doing certain things that were mathematical, such as placing objects in a line, or fitting things inside containers.

The photographs were a revelation to them. The set of photographs led to several discussions about her involvement and the schemas that she was currently displaying. Her mother, despite being very busy, became committed to observing Lyn at home and to providing data for a research project on young children's learning. Lyn benefited by being among interested and interesting adults who understood and supported her exploration of her environment both at home and at nursery.

This sequence shows Lynsey's deep interest in vertical trajectories

Different approaches will appeal to different adults. A skilled worker may tr
various ways of explaining or illustrating theories in order to reach a variety
of parents.

There are several nurseries throughout the UK and New Zealand that have
used schemas as a starting point for sharing ideas with parents about how
children learn. Many nurseries and schools throughout the UK have been
part of the Effective Early Learning Project and have used the Leuven
Involvement Scale as a tool to look at children's learning (Pascal and
Bertram, 1997). The important thing is to have a shared language **and** a
shared understanding of what young children are doing and learning.

Encouraging parents to share information

If you are open to listening to others, and prepared to share your knowledge
and to learn from them, then you may be ready to begin gathering
information about individual children that will enrich your relationship with
them and their families.

If this is a new way of working for you, you may choose to begin in several
different ways. However, one word of caution – **begin right away**. Do not
wait for everything to be perfect, or you may never get started.

STARTING POINTS

▶ Take some photographs of a child you know well and ask his/her
parents what they think he/she is doing.
▶ Consult the parents of a child you are struggling to provide for,
and ask for their suggestions. Be honest with them. They will
appreciate you recognising their greater knowledge of their own
child.
▶ Prepare a display and consult parents about which photographs to
include.
▶ Set up a small project and focus on one key issue. Ask parents to
meet with you each week to gather evidence of, for example, high
involvement or a particular schema.

You can probably think of lots of other ways to begin. It is helpful to keep
in mind two important aspects of working together with parents: informal
exchanges of information and shared record-keeping.

Sharing information informally

Sharing information verbally, on a daily basis, is often the way that parents and early years workers begin to get to know each other. Habits like always making a point of greeting each child and getting to know what helps him/her to settle and become involved, are useful in many practical ways for parents and workers. If you know that a child settles best out of doors on a favourite bike, then efforts can be made for it to be available.

On a home visit, the early years worker has an opportunity to see what the child does and how he/she reacts to the visit. Parents may supply a great deal of incidental information and this provides further material for future conversations.

A worker might meet the parent and child at the supermarket or cinema and, again, this provides shared experiences for future conversations. Children often think that workers live at nursery and will have lots of questions about what you are doing at the shops.

If there are opportunities to go out on trips with nursery children, you can learn a great deal about their interests. If parents go along too, then there is an opportunity for them to get to know you on a more personal level.

If you can capitalise on some of these informal ways of getting to know children and their families, then you are much more likely to be able to provide the right resources and support for the children at the right time.

Shared record keeping

Informal sharing of information about young children is useful up to a point. If it were possible to date and record these conversations about each child in some way then this would contribute, over time, to a record of the child's progress.

If what young children think, say, feel and do is taken seriously, then a record of each child's language and actions will offer a lot more information to adults and may result in more accurate predictions of what each child will do next.

To take things a stage further, if the worker watches a child at nursery and records in detail his actions and language, and the parent watches the same child at home and records his actions and language, then a fuller picture will inevitably emerge. Take for example, Henry, who was observed at home connecting all of the knobs on the kitchen cupboards with string, and also at nursery, playing with a train set and other construction toys. When staff and parents shared this information, it became clear that Henry's concern was with how things connect and what happens when they are connected together. Materials were provided so that he could extend his ideas about connecting, such as string, elastic, paper clips, Blu tack, glue, magnets, bikes and trailers, hooks, rope, needles, cotton, etc. His parents and workers were able to use language like 'fix', 'join', 'knot', 'bow', 'drag', 'pull', 'sew', 'stretch', 'long', 'shorter' and so on.

His parents and nursery workers have an opportunity to share their thinking with each other and to reach some new, shared understanding of Henry.

The records they collected showed that Henry was learning at a deep level. Without this information from home and from nursery it would have been more difficult to understand what his real interests were.

Just as it is very difficult to capture the moment when a child **knows** that three feathers is always three however they are arranged (in a line, clutched in one hand or floating through the air), it is difficult to capture other significant moments in the child's life. Detailed information about a child's involvement in carrying feathers around and arranging them in different ways enables us to understand what a child 'learning that three objects are always three objects' looks like. If parents and workers become better at recognising these sorts of moments then they can offer the right support to each child.

Benefits to children, parents and early years educators

Sharing ideas about the curriculum is about listening, watching and discussing. As a worker, you have learnt a great deal if you recognise the expertise of parents. Your attitude will have an impact. If you listen to parents then they will tell you more and you will understand the children better, so everyone involved will benefit.

Children benefit by having:

> ▶ support from the important adults in their lives, who are in tune with them and with each other
> ▶ resources offered for them to use when needed, for example a

coffee grinder, globe, mincer, whisk, when interested in 'rotating' objects

▶ all round support (i.e. at home and at nursery) for their social, emotional and intellectual development

▶ positive role models since their own parents will be actively engaged in studying them

▶ raised self-esteem, because their ideas are important to at least two significant adults.

Parents benefit by having:

▶ an opportunity to discuss and to be reassured about what their children do, on a daily basis

▶ the chance to speak with authority on a subject close to them, their own child

▶ the possibility of learning about theories of child development. They will be able to build on personal knowledge gained through practical experience.

Early years workers benefit by having:

▶ access to information from parents based on their intimate knowledge, understanding and insight about their own children

▶ an opportunity to discuss and negotiate a curriculum for each child based on his/her real experience and ideas

▶ a chance to inspire and support the parent in his/her search for new understanding

▶ a better opportunity to match the nursery curriculum to the needs of individual children.

Summary

▶ It is a good idea for parents and workers to share ideas about how children learn.

▶ There are several ways of sharing information, for example through a dialogue or through sharing visual aids such as photographs and video.

▶ Two developmental tools, which can be used to describe and interpret children's actions and are very useful to parents and workers, are the **Leuven Involvement Scale** and the search for recognisable patterns or **schemas** in children's actions.

▶ Early years workers must begin the dialogue with parents about children and encourage parents even though this may feel threatening to the worker's confidence in their professional knowledge.

▶ Children, parents and workers all benefit immeasurably when information is shared and detailed records are kept.

Bibliography

Arnold, C., (1990) Children Who Play Together have Similar Schemas. Unpublished dissertation (Certificate in Post Qualifying Studies).

Arnold, C., (1997) Understanding Young Children and Their Contexts. Unpublished MEd Dissertation, Leicester University.

Athey, C., (1990) Extending Thought in Young Children – A Parent – Teacher Partnership. London: Chapman.

Bartholomew, L. and Bruce, T., (1993) Getting to Know You. London: Hodder & Stoughton.

Bruce, T., (1991) Time to Play in Early Childhood Education. London: Hodder & Stoughton.

Gura, P. (ed.), (1992) Exploring Learning, Young Children and Block Play. London: Paul Chapman.

Laevers, F., (1993) Deep Level Learning. European Early Childhood Research 1, 53–68.

Laevers, F., (1994) The Innovative Project Experiential Education. Studia Pedagogica 16, 159–72.

Meade, A. with Cubey, P., (1995) Thinking Children. Wellington: New Zealand Council for Educational Research.

Nutbrown, C., (1994) Threads of Thinking. London: Chapman.

Pascal, C. and Bertram, A., (eds), (1997) Effective Early Learning. London: Hodder & Stoughton.

Rice, S., (1996) An Investigation of Schemas as a Way of Supporting and Extending Young Children's Learning. Unpublished MEd Dissertation, University of West of England.

Whalley, M. and the Pen Green Team, (1997) Report for the TTA on research project 'Parents' Involvement in their Children's Learning'.

4

Working with Parents who may be Hard to Reach

Getting to know the families

It is likely that whilst working in early years settings you will encounter families whose lives are going through a period of crisis or who are experiencing difficulties. They may well be involved with the health authority or social services. Children from these families will often have been 'referred' to a nursery or early years centre. A professional involved with the family can ask for a nursery place on behalf of the child or family, believing it to be in their best interest.

It takes time and patience to begin to understand what's going on in the lives of some families. Families function in very different ways. This chapter considers how to bridge the gap between nurseries and parents who may at first seem hard to reach.

Home visiting

One particular model of good practice in getting to know families is through home visiting. Home visiting can help all children and families, but especially those experiencing difficulties. Parents are often more relaxed and confident in their own homes and it is here that you gain valuable insight into family life. Children particularly seem to enjoy their 'special person in nursery' coming to visit them and sometimes a couple of home visits early on can help children who are having difficulty settling into nursery. These visits may also reassure their carers! (See chapters 2 and 8 for the importance of home visiting.)

It is important to home visit frequently when families are experiencing an unsettled period in their lives, especially when children are being brought into nursery via social services transport so you do not have day-to-day contact with their carers. The children in nursery who are least settled are those whose routines are constantly upset because of family crisis, so they don't get a chance to control their lives in any way. When working with families who are experiencing difficulties, where children's lives are fairly chaotic, it is often more effective to make short visits, calling round on the off-chance of catching them in rather than trying to arrange formal appointments. Most families welcome the chance to share news or photographs of their child and visits by nursery staff are usually seen very positively. Dates of meetings or reviews with other colleagues can best be passed on in person rather than by letter. Sometimes it may be necessary to visit at the weekend or early evening in order to find the family in. Staff in new integrated nursery settings or family centres may be able to negotiate time back when they make such visits. For childcare workers and educationalists in mainstream settings this may be more difficult.

Sharing information

Adequate and relevant record keeping is an essential part of the work of any early childhood professional. Parents need to be fully encouraged and enabled to contribute their expert knowledge on their child and help to maintain records. You need to bear in mind that many adults have anxieties about or difficulties with reading, writing and form-filling, and for some, English might not be their first language. You must be sensitive and creative in handling these issues. Taking any forms that need filling in into the family home can be helpful. You will need to explain the relevance of the information sought and then say something along the lines of: 'Some people have trouble filling in forms, are you okay with it or would you like me to help?'

Difficulties can then be openly acknowledged and ways found to work around them. For instance, if the child's first language is not English, you might have to ascertain whether anyone else in the family is able and willing to help read or translate for the parent. A translator from the community or a professional translator from within the social services department may be able to help. Any letter which might be sent home should always be read through and explained to the parent.

When families are from a cultural background or hold religious beliefs with which you are unfamiliar, it is important to firstly acknowledge this with the child's carers. You need to ask them to 'teach' you about their customs and practices. You need this information because it affects how you work with their children. When families are 'referred' by other agencies, you acquire background information about what's been happening in their lives. This is usually from the perspective of the social services team or the medical social work teams who make referrals. Of course it is important to take into account the information other professionals have compiled about each child and family, but it will always be just that – other people's views of how things are. It is critical that each family should have a chance to talk about what **they** think is happening in their lives. Regular home visits offer an opportunity for this to happen.

Good practice will ensure that all parents and carers are familiar with the nursery/family centre setting where their child attends and feel that they will be welcomed and supported whenever they visit.

Knowing the areas where families are living is important. You as the early childhood educator need to know where there are local shops and schools or where there is a shortfall of local services and amenities. Where families live in relation to their extended family and friends is also important. All this information will give you an important insight into factors affecting the family and the child. Reading the local evening paper can provide valuable information and gives you a 'feel' for what's happening locally. Being able to talk with parents about the area in which they live is often a good non-threatening ice-breaker.

A lot of parents have had very few, if any, experiences of being really listened to and there is a lot you need to learn from them. However, you have to be able to maintain clear boundaries in your work. It would not be appropriate for nursery workers to offer a counselling service. It is important to be clear with parents from the start that although you are willing to give them the time to talk, you can never offer total confidentiality. If you have any concerns about the well-being or safety of any child, you must share them with your manager and/or the social worker involved with the family.

Getting off to a good start

When your work is with families involved with social services or with children on the Child Protection Register, a lot of time inevitably seems to be spent in supporting parents in their efforts to work positively with their own social workers. It is worthwhile remembering that some families have grown up with social work involvement. Parents may have been in care themselves as children. Many parents grew up thinking that social workers were out there somewhere waiting to take them away. Not surprisingly, such ideas are hard to change. Although it might be flattering to the early years worker to be considered the 'goodie', it is not helpful in the long term. It would be inappropriate for you to collude with families and build up the idea of the social worker as the 'baddie'. Setting boundaries and maintaining them throughout the relationship is necessary for both your own and the parents' emotional and physical safety.

When children are placed on the Child Protection Register, the underlying aims of the social services department are always to establish consistency of care and develop an adequate system of monitoring the child's development. As an early years worker your task is to work with the family, enabling them to establish a routine whereby their child is getting to nursery on a regular basis. Occasionally this might even involve waking the family up in the morning, helping to get the child(ren) dressed and so on, or making determined efforts to find the family if they have missed a number of nursery sessions. This might involve home visiting outside nursery hours or visiting other family members/friends.

Helping families to fit in

However flexible the timing of sessions that are offered by early years services, most family centres/nurseries/playgroups tend to function on roughly an 8.30–9.00 am to 3.30–4.00 pm basis. There is still very little full-time provision for children under school age outside the private sector. For some families regular events do not exist. The time of day, even days of the week, have little or no importance. If no-one in your family or in your circle of friends goes out to work and if you have no children at school then the times you sleep, wake up, eat or socialise with friends assume very little significance. Families who function in this way have enormous difficulties 'fitting in' to the system. The system dictates that children need to be up, dressed and fed by a certain time in order to meet transport arrangements made by their social worker. For some families this may be impossible. Being back home in time to meet a child on his/her return, keeping appointments or remembering other big occasions may be very problematic for the families you work with.

It may be that you might want to organise your working routine in such a way that it will allow you to pick up children from their own homes. This is not always an easy thing to do, but establishing a routine for the child and family is so vitally important that it is worth making the effort.

If you are sincere in your commitment to working with these young children and their families you must convey to the carers that their family's welfare is important to you. You are offering their children something special – nursery education and care, a high quality early years experience. If you believe in the services you are running then it is worth making the effort to fetch their child and it is worth the family's effort to get up to get the child ready. What you are offering these parents is an alternative way of functioning as a family. By supporting them in their use of facilities, support groups for parents and so on, you are making it possible for them to access an important provision, where they will get support for themselves and experience for the children that can sometimes be life-changing. Reality dictates that sooner or later families will acquire the basic organisational skills necessary to get their child to school on a regular basis if they are to avoid trouble for themselves. It must be recognised that for some parents this task is monumental.

It is wrong to assume that all families will jump at the chance of quality nursery education or childcare: for many it is just another unwelcome intrusion into their lives. You need to be very sure that you have something really worthwhile and beneficial to offer to this family. It will be important to work very hard at 'selling' your services. However, the final choice on whether or not they want their children to attend lies with them – their lifestyle has to be their choice.

Early years educators may sometimes have to pick up children in the morning and take them home at the end of a session

Most parents want their child(ren) to have as good a life if not better than they had themselves. Our task is to help them recognise that quality nursery education is a step in that direction.

Building relationships

Too often families become known to professional agencies because of their tragedies or their vulnerabilities. Many have been labelled for so long that they have forgotten where their strengths and interests lie or have never been given the opportunity to discover them. As an early years professional you can work on and improve your 'natural' listening skills. You can encourage and enable parents and carers to talk about things they have done well, not just agonise over the problems they are experiencing being a parent. You can improve and deepen the relationship between nursery staff and parents. Parents and children may need help to improve their self-esteem. High self-esteem comes from:

> ▶ being acknowledged and appreciated for what you are doing successfully
> ▶ knowing you can trust people to be concerned about your feelings and needs
> ▶ feeling that the important people in your life are willing to give you time
> ▶ knowing that others will like your ideas and follow your lead
> ▶ being warmly accepted in your own world
> ▶ people's willingness to listen and take you seriously
> ▶ feeling that others enjoy being with you.

Cassie, a young woman with three children, was referred to a nursery as being from a family well-known in the community and to most professional agencies. She had a prison record, was involved with drugs from time to time and was now suffering from depression and was heavily involved with social services. Staff in the nursery got to know her better and offered her plenty of opportunities to talk – encouraging her to focus on her strengths. Cassie was able to tell her child's key worker how much and how far she and her young family enjoyed walking, often to parks in several areas of town. This was her strategy for coping when she felt low and it also benefited her children. She talked at length about how she enjoyed her work experience placement whilst at school which included working in an old people's home. She felt she got on well with old people and felt she had to. Talking together and she had a lot of patience with her recognising and sometimes drawing elderly neighbours. She was also on these strengths – all helped skilled in home decorating with a improve her self-esteem. Cassie talent for adapting bargains from the began to trust the nursery staff and local junk market for her home. She was able to ask for appropriate sup- was good at managing her benefit port for herself and her children money each week and could save if when she needed it, not just in times

Many of the parents that you work with in early years settings may have recently made huge changes in their lives. Many will want to improve their relationships with their children. Some will be interested in adopting a different kind of lifestyle or behaviour. It will be really important to help them think about how the other significant people in their lives are going to react to changes. Change is scary and often painful.

Susan, a very young mum whose Changing routines and taking back confidence had been built up over control was problematic for every- several months of working closely one. Katey had got used to doing with her key worker in nursery and things Grandma's way; Grandma had attending a support group for par- got her own special way of doing ents, decided that she wanted to take things which she thought was the more responsibility for bringing up best way of doing things. At first, her own child, Katey. Susan had left neither Katey or her Grandma most of the day-to-day decision- would accept the changes Susan was making to her child's grandmother. trying to make.

A particularly useful way of overcoming this type of hurdle is for nursery staff to forge an alliance with those family members or partners who could potentially cause problems. Often you find that once you have the granny or the grandad of the family on your side, relationships and progress in the work really begins. Making the effort to develop these relationships by taking any opportunity to invite carers into the nursery, spending some time getting to know them, and giving them as much information as they want will pay dividends in the end.

Children under stress

There are countless ways in which children living under stressful conditions show their feelings through their behaviour. As a nursery worker you need to know the child's context and then his/her behaviour makes perfect sense. What is really important is that you allow children the time, space and nurturing environment for them to wallow in play and make sense of things for themselves. As a trusted adult, you should see yourself as a facilitator in this healing process.

Security through routine

Children whose lives have no routine or who have no experience of tangible, consistent boundaries are often distressed. The children who are least settled in the nursery are often those who have not yet developed a routine in coming to nursery or whose routine has been upset in some way – either they come in late or have to be collected early. Sometimes they are brought in by someone different or miss sessions.

Security through routine

Many children have no experience of the security that routine can offer and find themselves dealing with upset in their nursery lives as well as having to cope with the various stresses at home. You can help this situation by providing the child with a nursery experience which is rich in quality and consistent in practice. One particular way of achieving this in a nursery setting is by structuring the session in the following way to incorporate:

> ▶ a welcome whereby one of the workers familiar to the child is always in a position in nursery to welcome the child when he/she arrives
> ▶ plenty of time to explore and play, with your support
> ▶ breakfast/snacks being available throughout most of the session whereby the children choose what and how much they want to eat and are encouraged to serve themselves
> ▶ a time to come together in a small group – this offers the children a time to get to know each other and develop friendships
> ▶ a lunch together – time to enjoy the social occasion and choosing your meal
> ▶ time at the end of the session to say goodbye to nursery staff and to other children
> ▶ taking home pieces of work children have made, notes for parents/carers and a time to confirm that you will see them again next session.

Often a child will ask to take a little something home from nursery (or sometimes a big something!) It is important to agree that she can take it then bring it back next time. The child then feels affirmed and knows that she is welcome to come back again.

Preparing children for change

It is vitally important to prepare children for any change. If you know of changes that are likely to happen in their home lives, a move out of the area, a parent going away or a child going into care, then you need to work together with the parents/carers on the best way to explain things to the child. Sardi, a family worker, remembers:

One of my saddest memories was of a three year old who sat on my lap and told me he needed to go back to his old house to get his bike – when I asked him the reasons why he said, 'I need my bike so I can look for my mum'. His mother had been in prison for four weeks and the friends and family caring for him thought it best not to explain or mention her to the child at all.

By writing to her in prison we were able to agree on a simplified but true explanation of where mummy was and from there we were able to assure him that one day she would come home.

One useful way of helping children cope with changes in their lives is by the use of photographs both on displays and made into special books for each child. Some nursery centres and day nurseries display photographs of their staff and the social services escort drivers that bring the children into nursery. They make books for the child featuring the many houses the child might spend time/sleep in, in the course of a week. You may just initiate discussions with the children in your setting about 'who's who' in their lives. In this way you can offer them the security of shared understanding.

'Care' for the carers

With the best will in the world, none of us is going to get it right every time. With every family you work with and however self-aware you are, there are times when working effectively is difficult. The particular characteristics of a family member may trigger off feelings that you are sensitive about. You must try not to become defensive and set up artificial barriers. Admitting you're stuck, you've run out of ideas, that you don't actually like this family is not easy but neither is it failure – it's life! What is of vital importance is that you talk about what is happening with someone else.

Good practice in early years education and care should ensure that all staff receive regular support/care load supervision from a senior member of staff. Currently this is much more likely to be offered in a social services establishment than in education or voluntary sector provisions. It may be hard in the private sector to take time out for this kind of in-service support, but staff in all settings will need some regular, consistent, individual feedback. It is important that you try to develop a personal support network, perhaps with a colleague within your setting. You can then provide each other with mutual support. A good general rule for working with any family is: if what you're doing doesn't seem to be working, talk about it honestly with someone whose judgment you trust. Then try another tack – anything else at all. At the end of the day you might have to let someone else work with the family and accept the fact that he or she might be able to work more creatively with them when it was not possible for you to do this. Again, that's not a failure – it's just a fact of life.

Getting involved as a worker

After working as a supply worker in the nursery, I started working alongside a colleague who was involved in a project at a nursery known as the 'Nurture Group'. This group provided care two mornings per week for children from 18 months upwards. The children came from families who were experiencing difficulties and were involved with social services in some way. Because of their age and the fact that the children and their families might be in need of a lot of support, the ratio was one worker to two children. All the children had special needs but some had more than others. Some are offered individual support in additional separate sessions.

Often our work involves supporting parents in their efforts to work with social workers to keep the family together. Many of the children were on the Child Protection Register and one of our first tasks was to enable the family to establish a routine whereby the child was getting into nursery on a regular basis. My co-worker and I regularly went out to collect children in the home if they missed their social services pickup; often this involved shouting through letter boxes to raise the sleeping occupants. Once they were awake and we were in the house we might have to search for the children's clothes or shoes around sleeping adults. We have both had a substantial amount of training in counselling skills which has stood us in good stead for this work. We both have the same belief in what we are offering to children which parents pick up from us. The families' welfare is important to use and we are offering their children something special – something worth us making the effort to fetch the child; something worth their effort to get up for.

For your own professional development and survival you need to recognise the fact that the children and families that you work with are not **your children** or **your families**, however much you might nurture and care for them and however much you disagree when colleagues appear to scapegoat a particular child/family for everything that goes wrong in the nursery. At the end of the day your relationship with them has to be professional. However much you may try to enable them to cope with and tackle difficulties in their lives, the power to change things for the better lies only within themselves. Young children of course do not have the same personal power and where they are caught up in stressful situations then the local authority may have to take on some responsibility for the child. The Children Act 1989 says 'the welfare of the child is paramount'. It states that 'children have a right to be informed, consulted and listened to' and any 'unnecessary delay in making decisions about children is harmful'. You as a representative of that authority must not be afraid to play your part responsibly if children are at risk or in need of additional help or support.

Record keeping

Good practice necessitates the keeping of up-to-date and accurate records of each child's achievement as well as their social, emotional and physical well-being. Early years workers will need to keep frequent detailed written observations of every child in the setting. These need to be really accurate and non-judgmental, particularly when children in your care in nursery are on the Child Protection Register or involved with social services in some way. You should share your own observations with the parents as you would with all children. However, you may also have to share them with the social services teams involved. As a key worker for a child in an early years setting you may well be asked to attend a core-group meeting for the particular child. These are held every six to eight weeks and take the form of a discussion between all the agencies involved with the family.

Endings

It would be naive and simplistic to assume that your intervention in the lives of the families you work with will always result in wonderful fairy-tale endings. Many families do go on to make changes for the better, some do not. On a bad day it may seem that all the care, encouragement and countless hours spent working alongside parents, helping them to recognise and make choices about their lives will have been to no avail. As an early years worker you need to believe that your work **does** make a difference and that the experience a child has now **will** affect them for the rest of their life. You may well have given the children in your care their first experience of consistent, thoughtful relationships with caring adults. In nursery they will have felt acknowledged as special little individuals where they were enabled to make choices about how they spent their time. Children and parents will inevitably move on from the nursery or early years setting. They may well forget about the centre and the names of their child's key worker but they will never completely forget those positive experiences. By working with parents and children in this way you are taking small steps towards breaking the cycle of family breakdown and child abuse.

Summary

▶ In most early years settings there will be parents who have spent most of their lives feeling like outsiders. Early years educators need to engage these parents and involve their children in nurseries to bring about a positive change in society. You need to become a 'resourceful friend' to these parents.

▶ Home visiting is an important way in to most families, but you must conduct these visits on the parents' terms, at times and in ways that suit the family's lifestyle.

▶ Even when parents appear to be making things difficult they are deeply committed to their own children 'getting a better deal'.

▶ As an early years educator it is important for you to work closely with colleagues from other departments. This does not mean that you have to be uncritical if other professionals behave inappropriately. It does mean that you have to be very clear about **your** roles and **your** boundaries.

Bibliography

Ferri, E. and Smith, K., (1996) Parenting in the 1990s. London: Family Policy Studies Centre and Joseph Rowntree Foundation.

Parenting Problems – A National Study of Parents and Parenting Problems. London: Family Policy Studies Centre.

Useful contacts

Family Policy Studies Centre, 231 Baker Street, London NW1 6XE (0171 486 8179).

Cry-Sis, London, WC1N 3XX (0171 404 5011).

Exploring Parenthood, 4 Ivory Place, 20a Threadgold Street, London, W11 4BP (0171 221 6681).

Homestart UK, 2 Salisbury Road, Leicester, LE1 7QR (0116 233 9955).

Meet-a-Mum Association, 14 Willis Road, Croydon, CR0 2XX (0181 656 7318).

National Newpin, Sutherland House, 35 Sutherland Square, London, SE17 3EE (0171 703 6326).

5

Working with Parents in the Home

This chapter is concerned with how students or nursery staff can prepare to work effectively with parents in the home. It deals with the issues of student home placements and early years workers visiting in the home. It also addresses the issues that arise for early years educators who are employed by parents as nannies.

As a student undertaking nursery nursing and childcare training programmes you are required by the awarding bodies to carry out practical training with children from birth to eight years in a range of placements. This may include working with young children in a home setting. Experienced staff in early childhood provisions are also often required to home visit and get to know the children who attend their nurseries in their home setting. Home visiting is seen as good practice by most early childhood educators, although many staff will not have had any training in home visiting. Even some experienced staff may not have a good understanding of what home visiting is about, or how it can work to benefit the children who have places in their nurseries. (See chapters 2 and 8 for the importance of home visiting).

Creating professional care givers

Training programmes can help students and experienced early childhood educators to feel confident as professionals. Courses need to combine theoretical knowledge and practical experience and should help students to:

> ▶ acquire new skills
> ▶ increase their knowledge and understanding
> ▶ build up their confidence
> ▶ have an opportunity to think about and sometimes modify the attitudes and beliefs that they have grown up with.

Practical training placements should help students and early years workers to:

> ▶ recognise their strengths and develop any existing areas of weakness
> ▶ develop self-awareness and assertiveness
> ▶ learn how to communicate with children and parents in their home setting.

If you are a student on a formal training programme you will be offered practical placements to facilitate your move from 'student or trainee' status to professional worker and equal partner. In some instances students move fairly quickly from being a trainee to the person with sole charge of a child.

Placements in the home setting

For students and early years practitioners undertaking placements in a home setting the challenge is to work effectively in what is often a very informal setting. You may already have had experience of working in a more structured and larger environment, such as a school or nursery, and have confidence in what you are offering to children in their nurseries. Home placements, however, involve you in responding to a less structured and predictable timetable. You have to relate much more on a one-to-one basis with parents. Some students and some experienced workers find this daunting and have expressed concerns such as: 'What if I don't like the family or they don't like me!' 'What should I do when the baby is asleep or during quiet times?' 'Will they expect me to know everything about feeding and other care routines?' 'What if they get angry about things that are going on in nursery and I'm on my own with them?'

Students undertaking placements in a school or a nursery don't generally have a great deal of contact with parents. You will normally be expected to refer parents on to the child's key worker, the nursery head or manager. Home placements are an important opportunity for you to engage fully with children and parents in their own environment.

Practical placements in the home setting are also an opportunity for you to experience different parenting styles and attitudes. Inevitably some students get placed with parents where there are very different family structures from their own. If this is your experience then it will help you to avoid the assumption that the children in your care will be getting a similar experience to your own. The placement may well encourage you to understand and recognise the role of parents as primary carers and educators of their child. It should also give you an understanding of what it means to work in an equal partnership with parents.

Principles to acknowledge

When working with parents and involving them in their children's education and care both students and experienced early years staff must acknowledge the following principles (O'Hagan and Smith, 1993).

> ▶ Parents are equal partners.
> ▶ Parents usually know more than anyone else about their child.
> ▶ Workers have a responsibility to involve parents.
> ▶ Workers should recognise and value the parent, parental culture, heritage and language.
> ▶ Parents have a right to be consulted on changes affecting their children.
> ▶ Parents have a right to negotiate with staff over issues affecting their children.
> ▶ Parents should be given every opportunity to understand what is going on and the rationale behind it, for example different types of play activity.
> ▶ Parents need encouragement in their parenting and a positive relationship with staff of all disciplines.
> ▶ Workers should recognise the need for confidentiality in dealing with parents.
> ▶ Parents sometimes need a break from their children.

Preparing for home placement

If you are about to undertake a home placement discuss it with your tutor or placement organiser. Once you have negotiated a suitable placement with them, get some details such as names, address, telephone number, ages of child/children and any other information which will help you conduct your first visit.

It is good to arrange an introductory visit prior to commencement of the placement. Visit at a time when you can meet the children and parents. Take along some information about yourself such as a personal profile. Parents might like to see what you have done in previous placements.

Students and NVQ candidates who have completed home placements have written 'survival guides'. They offer the following advice.

A survival guide

> ▶ Establish the ground rules on your first visit, such as start and finish times, what to do about meals, do parents have any objections to what you normally wear.
> ▶ Be honest with parents about what you hope to gain from the placement and what responsibilities you are expected to have and not to have.
> ▶ Find out what they expect of you.
> ▶ Tell the parents about your course and your previous experiences of working with children.
> ▶ Speak enthusiastically and confidently about your work with other children.
> ▶ Ask about their children.
> ▶ Explain to the parents the tasks and documentation you are required to complete.
> ▶ Assure them of your understanding of confidentiality.
> ▶ Seek permission to take photographs and use examples of their children's work.

Remember, you are a guest in their home. You will be sharing part of their private life and personal space. This must be respected. Small gestures like wiping your feet and taking off shoes indoors and offering to wash up the coffee mugs shows you respect their home. Be reliable. Turn up at the time and day you say you will. Parents may have arranged the day around you. Ring the placement and your tutor as soon as possible if you cannot attend.

Succeeding in your placement

The home placement is a valuable opportunity to decide if a career as a nanny or childminder is the right one for you. Feedback from parents and visiting tutors will help you decide whether you like the job and are well suited to it. Listen to what parents say to you about your skills and attitude to the children. What do they say about you to the tutor and their friends? Remember that parents who take students on may be looking for a qualified nanny and may use the opportunity of having a student in their home as a trial run. Your reputation as a caring and reliable worker may secure you a job with the family or with other families in the neighbourhood.

Although you will be working in a relaxed environment it must be viewed as a serious part of the learning programme. You must negotiate with your supervisor to complete certain tasks and fulfil the assessment criteria associated with the placement.

The placement provider will be asked to complete a report on your performance in placement. If possible the report form should be completed together. Use it as an opportunity to identify your strengths and weaknesses. Try to have a frank and open discussion about your performance. Value it as an instrument to measure your suitability to work as a nursery nurse in the home. Review your performance in college with your tutor and peers. You may wish to raise concerns with your tutor who will help you to resolve them. If problems with your practice are identified be prepared to discuss them openly and to accept constructive criticism. Both your tutor and placement supervisor will recognise that you are in the process of learning and developing your professional and personal skills and will not expect perfect practice. Do not be despondent if your end of placement report is not as good as you expected. Discuss it with your supervisor and tutor. An honest report that highlights your positive points and indicates areas of weakness is far more useful to your growth and development.

Preparing parents for supervising students

Training organisations have a responsibility to provide students with placements which offer them an optimum learning experience. Home placements provide a secure, supportive learning environment in an informal setting.

As well as this they require parents to become informal 'teachers' and 'trainers'. This may be a new experience for many parents who require preparation by college personnel. Recruiting suitable placement providers is the role of a placement organiser or tutor within the training organisation or college. Such individuals usually hold childcare and/or teaching qualifications. They will have an in-depth knowledge and understanding of the requirements of the course and the learning objectives associated with placement experiences. They will wish to get the balance right between meeting an individual student's needs and providing him or her with an optimum learning experience.

Tutors will probably try to schedule the home placement so that it coincides with the relevant theory taking place in college so that students have the necessary underpinning knowledge to support their practice in placement. As working in a home setting requires quite a high degree of developed interpersonal skills and confidence, the home placement should preferably be scheduled later in the course or training programme. It is useful if tutors know both students and providers so that they can match up personalities and similar social and cultural needs and expectations. At the same time, it will be important for you as a student to broaden your experience of families and family life styles.

Finding placements

Finding suitable home placement settings can be achieved by liaising with other professionals such as the Social Services Under 8s team, community midwives, health visitors, local childminders and qualified nannies. The placement organiser or tutor may visit parent and toddler groups, baby clinics and multiple birth support groups to tell them about the training programmes and the role of placement providers. Colleges may hold regular placement providers meetings to share information and develop good practice.

Placement settings will be approved by the college or training organisation based on guidelines laid down by the awarding bodies. This may include a visit by the placement organiser or tutor to approve the placement. Approval of a placement is based on the following criteria.

> ▶ The placement offers a high standard of childcare and education practice.
> ▶ It will adequately meet the needs of the children, student and others.
> ▶ Placing a student will not adversely affect the needs of the children, parents, student or others.
> ▶ Placement providers are fully aware of the assessment requirements of the training programme.

Stressful situations or ones that might put student, parent or child in danger must always be avoided. As students you have a right and responsibility to let your tutor or mentor know if you have been placed in a setting where the practice is bad, or you're experiencing difficulties.

In order for the provider and the student to gain the most from the placement, both must be prepared beforehand. This will involve negotiating the work placement objectives with the student and the provider.

Parents say that what they want from a student working with their children are that he or she must:

> - be able to use his or her own initiative and see when something needs doing
> - be confident in carrying out simple tasks
> - be relaxed and able to chat easily with adults and children
> - recognise when their child needs attention and comforting
> - be confident in asking when he or she is uncertain about something
> - fit easily into the family's routine.

It will be made clear to providers that they are acting in a supervisory role and they have a commitment to ensuring the student is working in a safe environment. Some organisations ask providers to sign a good practice contract, which stresses and reinforces the requirement for adequate supervision and safety. Figure 5.1 shows an example of a good practice contract.

Parents who undertake to have students in their home may have no previous formal teaching qualifications. They may be experiencing for the first time both the role of parent and the role of trainer. The feedback received most frequently from parents is that they are not always sure what tasks they are required to do with the students and whether the activities they are doing are adequate. Providing written information about the types of tasks and experiences students are required to undertake is very useful. This could take the form of an information booklet.

In their role as placement provider parents will wish to have time to talk to and teach their student as well as to have fun. Children, parents and students can gain an enormous amount from working together. Most parents find the experience very rewarding and wish to repeat it.

Positive comments from parents at the end of the student's home placement include: 'I don't want her to leave, how did I ever manage without her?'

'We were able to do things with the children that I cannot normally do on my own, such as swimming, shopping and outings to the park.'

WORKPLACE CONTRACT

(STUDENT) I AGREE....

- To arrive in plenty of time to prepare activities.
- To be punctual at all times.
- To stay and ensure all the jobs are completed and to be flexible.
- To maintain confidentiality.
- To be aware of placement rules and policies.
- To help maintain a safe and secure environment.
- To act responsibly and with initiative at all times.
- To dress appropriately.
- To be aware of daily routines.
- To communicate effectively with adults/children.
- To be friendly, helpful and willing.

SUPERVISOR (I AGREE)....

- To do everything that is reasonably practical to ensure the health and safety of the student.
- To accept the student into my home and take responsibility for the student whilst caring for my child/children.
- To supervise the student at all times.
- To make the student feel welcome.
- To offer support, guidance, advice and constructive criticism.
- To give opportunities for the student to have non-contact time in order to evaluate and assess observations/activities.
- To assess/evaluate the student's work and sign as required.
- To involve the student in the daily planning and routines.

SIGNED: STUDENT ....

                SUPERVISOR ....

                DATE ....

Figure 5.1 A workplace contract

'She did things with the children that I would not have the time or confidence to do, like lots of creative activities and cooking activities.'

'The children have become very fond of him and he's now invited back to their celebrations.'

'She worked with the toddler which gave me valuable time to get to know the baby.'

Children, parents and students can gain an enormous amount from working together

'She involved me in her written work and made me feel my experiences as a parent were skills I could pass on to her.'

The parent as employer

Parents who employ nannies do so because they want their child(ren) cared for in their own home. Parents want someone who will be dedicated to their child. They may have no previous experience of being an employer and often know very little about the practice and legal implications of employing a person in their home. One parent commented: 'I wanted to work in partnership with someone who would love my children like I do. I suddenly became an employer but I was very clear that I was not employing a servant but someone who would put the best interests of my children first. I had to examine my skills to see if I had the right ones to make a good employer.'

Parents may feel that the care of their children is their most important priority. They may be willing to pay the maximum amount to secure the best quality service. Parents will often choose a qualified nursery nurse or childcare worker because of their years of training and knowledge. The duties they expect of a nursery nurse will relate only to the care of the children. Care in the home can also be conducted by a mother's help or au pair. They may have no formal childcare qualifications and could be expected to take on household duties as well as child care.

Some parents plan to employ a nanny in advance of the actual need. It may be planned to coincide with a return to work or the arrival of a second child. Parents may employ nannies on a part-time basis and use it as a trial period to assess whether they could work in their home with another person sharing the care of their children.

Recruiting and selecting a nanny is a complex and serious process. Agencies exist to help parents find suitable nannies or mother's helps. They can be supportive, especially for new parents who are engaging a nanny for the first time or if they need a nanny at short notice. Agencies will charge a fee to parents for this service.

The selection process can be as formal or informal as parents wish. If an agency has been used the applicants will already have been screened by them. Parents may wish to have several meetings with prospective nannies. They will usually involve the children in the meetings. If possible parents will want to know what the children think of the nanny. The children's reaction to the potential employees can influence their decision. Parents may involve grandparents or a nanny currently in post. They are not necessarily looking for someone who has passed the training programme with flying colours. What they want is:

> ▶ someone who is confident
> ▶ a person who can use his or her initiative
> ▶ someone who shares the same values and has the sort of personality which will mesh with their family.

Parents will want to take up references and will usually go to the college where the candidate trained to get a reference. Parents will want to know something of the candidate's background and may question him or her at the interview. They will be interested in placement reports and evidence of work done with children in practical placements.

Some parents will favour candidates who share similar values to themselves, such as religious or cultural beliefs. Parents may be vegetarians and will need to be reassured that their children will not be fed meat.

One parent commented that she needed to have total trust in her nanny. She needed to be able to have someone in her home whom she trusted sufficiently to have her treat it as her own home.

A trial or probationary period allows parent and nanny to explore together their shared values and beliefs. This probationary period is for **both** parties. Parents may use this as a time to model their approach to parenting for the nanny. Some parents will spend time at home with the children and nanny during the early days. One newly qualified nanny reported that she found having the mother at home but in the distance very reassuring and helped her to learn the routine the baby and parents favoured.

The parents' role as employer is a very responsible one. They should draw up a contract of employment between the nanny and themselves. It should set out clearly what is expected of the nanny. A contract contains

Together, the parents and nanny need to agree what duties the nanny is expected to carry out

information on the conditions of service and should state the title of job, hours of work, rates of pay, holiday and other benefits. Together the parents and nanny need to agree what duties the nanny is expected to carry out on a regular basis. Both parents and nanny will want some degree of flexibility built into the contract. It is a vital instrument for clarifying who is responsible for what. A contract also establishes a mutual understanding of the roles and responsibilities of employer and employee.

Parents need to know about taxation, payment of superannuation and insurance. A useful source of information is the Inland Revenue office. Parents may advise their nanny to join a professional body and to contribute to a pension scheme.

The nursery nurse as employee

A nursery nurse seeking a position to work as a nanny can register with an agency, respond to a local or national advertisement or gain a position through a personal contact. Nursery nurses are advised to apply for more than one position and to attend several different interviews.

You will need to prepare an up-to-date curriculum vitae (CV) with the names of two referees. Have several references and placement reports available to take to interviews as well as samples of work carried out with children during your training programme. Ask to meet the children and to speak to the previous nanny if appropriate. Visit the family several times if necessary. Be honest about your range and depth of experience. It is likely you will develop job application skills during your training programme at college. Seek help with writing letters of application, preparing a CV and interview techniques. Your tutor may arrange talks from practising nannies, parents who employ a nanny, employment agencies and representatives from professional bodies.

Nannying is often a student's first job on qualifying from college. Some students start the job on a part-time basis to allow both themselves and the parents to determine if the job is right for them. The opportunity to work as a nanny provides an excellent opportunity to work in close partnership with parents. Qualified nursery nurses who take on a nanny role want to be closely involved with parents in making decisions about the care of their children. They are individuals who feel confident enough to make, if necessary, sole decisions about the care of the children for whom they are responsible. The transition from student to practitioner with sole charge of young children can be daunting. A settling-in period when the parents are at home with the nanny is reassuring for both parents and nanny. It is a very useful time for identifying expectations.

A good idea is to create a handbook which contains lots of information about the children, their routines, their likes and dislikes concerning food, and so on. This should be created by the parents and can be maintained by the nanny who could pass it on to any incoming nannies. The nanny has a responsibility for gathering information for the parents. This may relate to events at school, visits to the clinic or doctor's surgery. The nanny may attend school or nursery events with or without the parents.

Maintaining a day book is an excellent way of communicating to parents what has occurred during the day. It creates a focus of conversation and makes parents feel that they have had a share of the child's day too. The child can also see that parents are involved in their day. This is particularly useful for school children who may wish to relate incidents and events which happened at school.

One nanny described her role in the family as: 'Mother for the day. You have to be confident and assertive without being too dogmatic. You have to get the balance right between using initiative and not taking over.'

Nannies play a key role in the child's life. They may make decisions about when to buy the child new shoes or a winter coat or if the child's cold warrants a doctor's appointment.

Organising time with children requires a great deal of flexibility. Planning the day has to contain outings that a parent would plan for their child's experience. After-school activities require a degree of flexibility about start and finish times. Nannies and parents need to build in flexibility which takes care of unplanned events. Abuse of this flexible approach to working by either party can destroy the working relationships between nanny and employer. The child will also take part in the nanny's day. She may have to keep appointments to the dentist or bank. Such activities can be made into adventures for the child too.

Working together in the home allows parents and nannies to become friends. This positive relationship can be sustained for many years even after the nanny moves on to another job. If nanny and parents are able to conduct open and frank discussions on issues such as rewarding good behaviour and dealing with inappropriate behaviour, the messages to the children will be clear and coherent. The nanny needs to identify her own feelings and values about acceptable standards of behaviour. It is necessary to respect the parents' values and beliefs without compromising her own views. She may object to certain tasks or activities on religious or ethical grounds. Nursery nurses who work full-time with children and who are with them from birth play a vital role in developing the child's personality and character.

Working as a nursery nurse in a private home can be a lonely job, particularly if it is a rural setting away from the nanny's own neighbourhood and if the parents work long hours. Parents may know of other nannies working in the area. There may be a local nanny group – if not, consider setting one up. Go along to parent and toddler groups or activity clubs. Get to know the health visitor and find out what is happening for children in your area. Nursery nurses enjoy the opportunity to speak with other nursery nurses to share ideas and concerns.

It is important that once qualified, you continue to practise the skills learnt in college and to keep up to date with new developments in childcare and education. Look into new training opportunities and short courses that might fit in with the job.

Summary

- ▶ All early years educators need training in how to work effectively in the home setting.
- ▶ Early years educators need to value the strengths and acknowledge the needs of parents.
- ▶ When working in the home or conducting home visits staff need to be very clear about their boundaries.
- ▶ Early childhood educators must learn to listen to parents.
- ▶ Parents supervising students on placement need to be given a clear understanding of their role.

Bibliography

Bruce, T. and Meggitt, C., (1996) Child Care and Education. London: Hodder & Stoughton.

O'Hagan, M. and Smith, M., (1993) Special Issues in Child Care. London: Ballière Tindall.

6

Supporting Adults Who Feel Let Down by the Education System

Education is a major determinant of lifelong opportunities (Flynn, 1986).

Many adults grow up feeling that they were let down by the education system and were not encouraged to fulfil their learning opportunities. When they become parents they are often very concerned that their children should do better. They want to be supportive parents. Some of the parents in your setting will want to increase their own skills in literacy and numeracy. This chapter describes how important it is that there should be a number of different access routes for parents who want to become adult learners in any community. Early years settings have a strong tradition of supporting adults wanting to return to learning and they have a key role to play. Parents with young children need to feel confident and have a sense of their own competence as learners if they are going to be able to support their children's learning needs. In your setting even if the main focus is on daycare or nursery education it is still important for you to point parents in the right direction so that they can get into adult basic education classes or on courses that may help them with their parenting.

An individual's right to an education

It is now generally accepted that the state has the duty of providing education for all its children. However, it was not until 1880 that elementary (primary) education was made compulsory. Secondary education was left practically untouched by the state until the beginning of the 20th century and then was only available to a small percentage of the population. It was not until 1944 that the Education Act required local authorities to provide suitable secondary education for all pupils. Towards the late 1960s a comprehensive system of education was set up with the aim that all children would begin their secondary education with equal chances of success.

However, students still leave school in this day and age with no formal qualifications and many find it difficult to find any permanent employment. Unemployment often reinforces young people's feelings of low self-esteem and a lack of confidence.

Further education colleges offer places to students of sixteen or over but students who have had an unhappy time at school are often not motivated to take on further study. They may feel cast out into a world of unemployment with no hope of changing their lives.

Why parents feel let down by the education system

Some of the parents using your nursery may have gone through the education system with very little parental support. This is not because their parents did not care, but because they in turn may have had negative experiences of school. The parents in your centre may well feel that they 'failed' at school. Parents often say that from the beginning of their secondary school they had counted the days until they could go out to work. They remember vividly all the different excuses they used for **not** going to school. Those who could successfully 'wag it' and stay out of school often had high status among their peer group. Some families would not have been able to afford to keep older children at school. In many families work is still seen as more valuable than further education, although with changes in the state benefits system young people now feel 'forced' to stay on.

Often parents will not have experienced difficulties until they reached secondary school. Their memories of primary school are generally very positive. However, the transition from a smaller primary school situated in a familiar community to a large comprehensive school can be traumatic. Students with low self-esteem and with limited parental support can find it bewildering and difficult to relate to the different organisation and expectations of secondary school. The support they do find is invariably through a peer group of similar students all of whom find the system difficult to cope with and who have no motivation to learn. Some of the parents who come to your nursery will have vivid memories of dropping out of school and of being part of a group that was constantly getting into trouble.

Family breakdown can lead to difficulties at school. Some students are expected to care for younger siblings if their parents are working an evening shift. Conditions at home might not be conducive for doing homework with no quiet place to work if the house is overcrowded. Parents using your nursery, particularly mothers, may have had to cope with caring for younger siblings or even caring for their own parents. They may not have been involved in any real studies at school.

Poverty can be an isolating factor – for example, parents might not be able to afford the right books or the PE kit that is deemed so important in secondary schools. To be different from one's peers is a definite obstacle at senior school. Some of the parents in your nursery may have vivid memories of feeling that they didn't fit in. This may make it hard for them to trust you and other staff when their children come into nursery.

Students from different minority ethnic groups, where English is not their first language, often experience difficulties especially if their parents in turn do not read or write in the English language. These students are as able academically as other students but often fail to get the support they need and are stereotyped as 'under achievers'. Some of the parents in your setting may not feel confident using English as a spoken or written language.

The teacher's attitude and approach is an important factor in how pupils feel about school. Adults who have been let down by the education system often say, 'I was made to feel stupid'. You may have to work very hard to support parents who use your nursery if they felt like this at school. You can help parents to rebuild their low self-esteem and develop confidence in their ability to help their own children.

Pupils with special needs can be so easily left behind with large classes and limited resources. If any of your parents have had learning difficulties at school they may well be very anxious about their own children's progress.

From the age of twelve Trudy, a nursery parent, didn't feel confident at school. She had many friends, but didn't feel able to ask at home for help with homework. Her grandmother had been her carer since the age of nine due to family breakdown. Her grandmother struggled with literacy and felt that keeping the home and family together was her priority. On numerous occasions a particular teacher humiliated Trudy in front of the whole class. She was made to stand at the front and recite work over and over again. Through this negative experience of continually being 'put on the spot' Trudy became disempowered. She lost confidence in herself, felt useless, and this led to a loss of interest in her own education. She said she 'couldn't wait until the day she was able to leave school and work in a factory'.

Building relationships with parents as learners – establishing trust

In early childhood settings it is really important to develop relationships between parents and workers which are based on trust. Parents need to know that staff care about them as well as their children.

It is easy to make assumptions about people, by the way they look, talk or behave. For example, a parent with a physical disability using a nursery talked of people assuming she was 'stupid' because she had difficulty speaking without dribbling.

Parents coming into nursery or reception classes often talk about the difficulties they are experiencing with their children's schools. Their own negative experience has made them fearful of talking to their child's teacher in case they can't cope with what is said. They don't go to parents' meetings, consequently they are seen by teachers as not caring, and a vicious circle is set up. Schools assume that they are either uncaring or uncommitted and misinterpret parents' behaviour: 'those parents we'd like to see just never come in'.

Through getting to know the parent as an individual, early years workers gradually become aware of their particular needs. For example, an unemployed parent might be dismissed as 'idle' when in fact they might be struggling to find work because they have a difficulty reading and writing.

Even filling in an application form can be tortuous for some parents. It is offputting for parents if they are bombarded with too much information too soon.

Parents sometimes appear aggressive or over-confident to hide their fears of confronting their own learning difficulties. They might joke about 'not having any qualifications for anything'.

As early years workers, it is important to be aware of small clues. You need to be non-judgmental and supportive. A parent who used one early years centre for many years built a strong relationship with his key worker and began to speak about his partner's difficulty with literacy. He then gained enough trust to ask for help for himself.

Addressing individual parents' needs

Once a position of trust has been reached it is easier for early years educators to establish exactly what the individual parent's learning needs are. This could be achieved through a series of discussions with the parent, allowing him or her to make choices about what particular area of education to have help with initially. A time would need to be set aside for parents to come in for this purpose. The meeting would need to be as informal as possible, and unlike a school setting where the teacher is on one side of the desk and the student on the other.

It is paramount that early years workers have an understanding and knowledge of the options available to parents who want to improve their literacy and numeracy skills.

There are usually services available at local further education colleges for adult learners. This includes adult basic education one-to-one tuition which could be provided in the privacy of the learner's home if preferred.

Occasionally in primary or secondary schools, family literacy projects are set up where parents can get some support. **Remember that parents may find it extremely difficult to admit to difficulties with literacy.**

Sheila is 28 and has two children aged seven and five. She missed school often when she was young because she was expected to stay at home and look after her younger brothers and sisters. Education was not seen as important in her household. Working to earn money to support the family was vital.

Sheila can read and write but is already struggling to help her seven year old daughter with her school work. She always appeared aggressive and looked embarrassed when approaching staff. She was reluctant to join a group at first but said she would come along to give it a go.

At the first session she was met by the tutor half way down the stairs on her way out again, too nervous to join the others. Once in the room she could not stop talking and was very anxious.

Through her participation in the group, Sheila has become more confident in herself. She now appears much more relaxed. She is not afraid to ask for help and advice from teachers. Her organisational abilities have become apparent and she took on paid work in the crèche and was popular with all the parents. She began work as an evening cleaner and felt confident enough to ask for a Thursday evening off in order to keep attending the course.

Sheila was fortunate enough to attend a three-day residential course held at a local conference centre. She was very reluctant to go when first approached, but afterwards said 'It was the best three days of my life!'.

Evelyn, an Afro-Caribbean parent with a child in nursery, spoke with a member of staff about her concerns for her youngest son going to school. Her oldest child had struggled with literacy and she had felt unable to support him. She wanted to avoid this happening again with her younger son. Eventually, after several informal chats with the member of staff, Evelyn spoke about her own difficulties.

- She had missed a lot of school due to the fact that she had had to care for eight brothers and sisters when her mother died.
- She was unable to spell.
- She found it difficult to construct sentences.
- She avoided writing.
- She felt unable to attend parents' evenings in case she could not understand what the teacher was saying.

Evelyn was enthusiastic about the thought of attending a family literacy project but unfortunately became frightened about what people would think. Her family had already suffered racist abuse and humiliation in a community where the majority of adults were white.

It is important that the choices are made clear to parents and that parents make a commitment to getting involved in their own time and their own way. When addressing parents' learning needs it is important that we start with small steps and regular reviews are made of parents' progress. It may be offputting to ask the parents to commit themselves to an extensive learning programme. Modular or short-term courses are easier and more accessible for adults returning to education second time around. For example, a commitment for six weeks can give the parent a taster. The parent can then opt to withdraw from the course if it is not what he or she expected.

NVQ programmes allow parents to work at their own pace

Courses with examinations at the end may be daunting for parents who feel let down by the education system. They may prefer courses such as City and Guilds Word Power which has three different stages: Foundation, Stage 1 and Stage 2. Students can access the course at different stages and the materials are broken down into units and elements. There is no right or wrong way to work through them so that students can go at their own pace and choose the units they feel most confident with first.

NVQ programmes which lead to a qualification for work, for example with young children, allow ongoing assessment and accreditation which will allow parents to work at their own pace and make the decision to be assessed when they themselves feel ready.

Setting up a basic skills group

If parents have expressed a need, and are willing to put their trust in you and feel comfortable in your establishment, you could set up a group or course to help meet their learning needs.

Initially you have to establish that there are enough parents interested in the proposed project/group.

You may decide that more than one group is needed, for example you might decide to run a single sex group as well as a mixed gender group. In one nursery setting men made it clear that they did not want to admit to their lack of literacy skills in a mixed group (see chapter 9). The same can be true for some women.

You will need to take time to consider the shift patterns of your working parents. It is important to set up your group/course at a time when as many people as possible would be able to attend regularly. Ideally other agencies, such as the local further education college, would be involved from the beginning as this would give a wider community interest and ensure the group had the maximum support. It is beneficial to draw on as wide a pool of experience and ideas as possible.

Setting up a new group will always involve some costs in terms of resources, staff, salaries, travel costs and administration. You will need to have a room and resources to hold a crèche for the children to use. You will also need to decide whether you will run the group during the school holidays. If so, you will need to set up a playscheme for older children in the holiday period.

As a community nursery, family centre, playgroup or school, funding for an adult education project might not be available from your budget, so funding for the group or project would have to be found from other agencies. The Government funds the Basic Skills Agency precisely because of the upsurge in demand for family literacy groups and projects in the last few years. There are many local, national and European initiatives, such as the European Social Fund, which may sponsor such schemes as it recognises how important parental support is to children's learning. It may be possible to provide transport for participants or pay their travel expenses through European funding (see chapter 10). Applying for funding can be a time-consuming process but it is rewarding in the long run. It is an easier process if application for funding is undertaken along with other organisations. You may be able to link up with several other community-based resources and put in a joint application.

Once funding has been secured a steering committee should be set up, consisting of all the organisations involved. If a joint project is agreed between, for example, a nursery school, a primary school and a further education college, then all these organisations would need to be represented on the management committee. It is vital to include parent representatives on the committee as they can offer an alternative and practical insight into what needs to be offered. After all, the project is for parents! The committee would have to meet regularly to review the project, and provide the funding agencies with feedback on how the project was developing. It can be useful when you are setting up a project to visit well-established projects in other areas to share ideas and ways of working. It helps to know what has not been useful or successful in other projects as this could well save you time and unnecessary effort.

Running a basic skills (literacy and numeracy) group is not difficult but the staff and volunteers involved will need appropriate training to equip them with the skills to teach and encourage adult learners. They would need to learn specific teaching methods and ways of assessing the adult learner's progress. They would also need to learn about appropriate resources for the project and how to access them, for example with regard to disabled learners and learners for whom English is not their first language.

If you are interested in setting up this kind of a group then you should contact the local Adult Basic Education department. They will give you details of courses available to equip you with these skills.

Qualifications to work with parents

Nursery nurses in a number of early years settings have gone on to undertake the Certificate in Education in Post Compulsory Education course to gain the necessary qualification to teach adult learners. This can be useful additional training for an early childhood educator particularly if in the future you want to work in one of the integrated early years centres which have a focus on adult needs as well as children's education and care. For example, nursery nurses in Leeds now run a very exciting and innovative project, The Home Learning Partnership, within the Leeds Education 2000 Early Learning partnership. The Home Learning Partnership produces a pack called 'Getting Started'.

Designing a parent study group

The individual parents' learning needs have to be considered carefully when designing the framework of a short course or project.

Since many of these parents will have low self-esteem and feel fairly powerless it is crucial to include assertiveness and self-esteem within the training. Always give the parents time to relax, time to speak and listen. Never 'put them on the spot'. Do not be afraid to stick to a planned agenda, but always remember you need to be flexible and open to parents' needs.

It is useful to break the course down into small modular sections where parents can choose to be part of a 'roll on, roll off' way of working and learning. This allows parents to continue with their family and/or work commitments and still allows them the chance to gain credits towards their education.

It is important not to have too large a group of learners and to have volunteers as well as a tutor in order to encourage and offer support in pairs or as individuals throughout a session. Up to eight learners is the optimum size for their needs to be met and the group to function well.

Aims and objectives

Before the group starts you will have to have some clear learning outcomes in mind. This can be done by identifying the course aims and objectives.

Up to eight adult learners is the optimum size for the group to function well

Some aims and objectives may seem a small step to you but would be a huge learning objective for some parents. For example, you might ask parents in your group to set some time aside to visit the local college to seek information about what courses were available. For parents who have failed at school, visiting a local college would be a fairly daunting experience. It is essential that parents have some immediate experiences of success. Courses or projects should be a mixture of practical experiences, writing and discussion-based exercises. In this way you will cater for the needs of all those involved in the group. Some people find it easy to talk, while others prefer to write and those with a creative flair may enjoy practical experiences such as making story sacks for their children. (Story sacks are large bags with a drawstring through the hem in which soft toys or models relating to certain children's book are kept together with the book.)

Recruitment

Ideally recruitment should be by 'word of mouth'; individual approaches work best. Even if parents are able to read a poster advertising a group they might be too nervous to approach staff about it.

Chat to parents about what is available and show that you understand how they are feeling about taking such an important step as joining an adult learning group. The group should ideally take place in a centre where learning already takes place, such as a nursery. Other local community resources and schools should be encouraged to talk to their parents about the group. You may want to involve parent governors and community representatives in handing out leaflets about the group at parents' evenings or community meetings. Ideally, representatives would also be prepared to talk about the group at such events.

Posters should be designed with clear print and key words without being too simplistic as this could cause offence. A diagram or cartoon makes the poster look friendly and inviting. The poster should have names of the workers to contact for more information, with photos if possible, where the group is to take place, what it will be about and when it will take place. If you are able to offer additional services, for example a crèche, this should be specified on the poster. The local evening newspaper and free papers could be contacted with details of the project for maximum publicity.

Very anxious adult learners may appreciate a home visit so that they can discuss their learning in familiar surroundings and not feel threatened or intimidated in any way. It may give them more time to think about whether or not it is the right option for them and the right time to embark on something new.

Nurseries which have recruited fathers have found that whilst men seem reluctant to attend 'groups' they respond better if they are invited to 'workshops' which don't require long-term commitment. A male tutor or volunteer may be needed to encourage men to attend.

Setting the scene

For parents who have had negative experiences of school and the school regime, the atmosphere for learning must be informal and comfortable. If a parents' room is not available in your setting, perhaps you could use the staffroom.

The room should be set out to be inviting and homely. Time should be spent carefully planning how to make the room warm and welcoming. A bare room can be very clinical and threatening. Armchairs need to be set in a circle to promote discussion. A dining table is useful for everyone to work at. Refreshments should be offered when group members arrive as this puts people at their ease, allowing them to adjust to the setting and helping to 'break the ice'. Time needs to be allowed for an exchange of dialogue between group members, for reflection and a gentle start to the session.

Practical resources

Many of the parents joining adult learning groups will be extremely nervous and may not be aware of the resources needed. It would be useful if you could provide a 'return to learn' pack containing the necessary practical resources needed for the course, for example lined notepaper, pens, pencils, prittstick, erasers. In one nursery parents were provided with a small art file containing essential stationery items. This became known as a 'briefcase' and was carried with pride to every session. The staff had not anticipated the full impact this resource would have on the parents. They were empowered in their learning right from the start and felt valued. This was the first time some parents had owned the correct equipment for a class. This encouraged other parents to ask about the course; they were intrigued about what was inside the briefcase.

One parent, who was placed into care as a child when her mother died and who had attended a school for children with special needs, had many difficulties with literacy. She was particularly proud of her brief-case. She carried it faithfully to every session and kept it 'on top of the wardrobe' so she knew where it was. She enjoyed having somewhere of her own to keep her pens and paper, probably for the first time in her life. She 'personalised' it with her name and with stickers.

Books chosen for the course are equally important. Although some parents may be struggling with basic skills, it is not appropriate to use textbooks that have been designed for children. Adult textbooks are available and these should be carefully selected with consideration given to gender, ethnicity and disability. A junior dictionary, however, is easier to follow than an adult one. It may also be useful for parents to compile their own dictionaries in little notebooks. For disabled learners, resources such as pen grips are available through the adult education departments of local further education colleges.

If workshop activities are planned for the course, sufficient materials need to be available to give learners a choice of activity. For example, in a creative workshop there needs to be a wide selection of resources such as paint, clay and modelling materials.

A small charge may be necessary but must be kept to a minimum so as not to exclude parents on low incomes from the workshop experience.

Attendance certificates, printed specially with the parent's name, are often very much appreciated and valued. This may be the very first time their learning has been acknowledged with a certificate.

Establishing links between learning organisations

A solitary project in a nursery or playgroup might be isolated and financially vulnerable. Establishing links with other learning organisations can be very important in terms of sharing knowledge, experience and resources. Through linking closely with a local college the course would gain recognition and could be formally accredited through an awarding body, such as City and Guilds, NVQ, RSA or NOCN. Staff from the college can offer advice, have access to resources and are aware of further courses. They may be able to secure funding to support projects or courses through the Further Education College or the Training and Enterprise Council, for example. Through links with the local colleges, learners may be offered opportunities to attend residential courses at minimal cost. Residential courses offer activities which can be accredited and which are also enjoyable. It is also a great opportunity for parents to meet other learners from other centres.

It is useful to arrange links with local schools to pool resources and share common knowledge about parents' needs. Schools may have computers which parents could access for a technology workshop. Schools are increasingly being expected to involve parents. They may also have space available to run a course.

USING LIBRARIES AS A RESOURCE

The local library is an invaluable resource to link with and one which parents might not have had the confidence to access themselves. A trip could be organised to the library as part of the group's activities. Staff at the library would be informed beforehand of the visit and could tell parents about the facilities available and make them feel welcome and able to join. Parents are sometimes worried that their children will 'spoil' books if they borrow them from the library, but library staff could reassure parents about this.

Libraries are a source of information with which learners might not be aware. Once links have been established libraries could prove invaluable in terms of borrowing books for parents and their children. It is important that children see their parents as readers and see books as familiar items at home as well as at nursery and school.

Summary

▶ For those parents who feel that they failed first time around a second chance allows them an opportunity to achieve something for themselves. A small achievement is a major step forward for those who feel they have never succeeded. Adult learners will feel pride in being committed to learning when in the past they did not feel any commitment to school. Once they feel achievement is within their reach, parents will become self-motivated and want to learn more.

▶ When they are given a second chance to learn, parents develop

greater self-esteem and will become more confident in themselves. They will start to believe in themselves and feel more positive about their future prospects.
▶ When they feel confident themselves, parents will be able to help their children learn and will feel better able to approach teachers for advice and to give appropriate and critical feedback. They will become confident enough to speak up for their children and their children's needs and if necessary will become advocates on behalf of their children.
▶ By being offered a short-term group/course they may go on to be involved in a local adult basic education group, attend a college course, seek employment, attend school meetings for the first time. Each individual parent will move on at his or her own pace.

Bibliography

Alexander, T., Bastiani, J., Beresford, E., (1995) Home–School Policies – a practical guide. Nottingham: Jet Publications.

Getting Started, (1997) Leeds: Home Learning Partnership.

Hannon, P., (1995) Literacy, Home and School: Research and Practice in Teaching Literacy with Parents. London: The Falmer Press.

Flynn, P. (ed.) (et al.), (1986) You're Learning All the Time: Women, Education and Community Work. Nottingham: Spokesman.

Useful contacts

The Basic Skills Agency, 1–19 New Oxford Street, London WC1A 1NU.

Home Learning Partnership Leeds Education 2000, The Burton Business Park, Hudson Road, Leeds LS9 7DN (0113 280 6662).

National Home School Development Group, Dr John Bastiani, 67 Musters Road, Ruddington, Nottingham NG11 6JB (0115 984 5960).

A useful case study called 'Small Bears and Philosophers: Ideas Underlying Practice in Early Years Settings' is available from: CEDC Family Education Unit, Lyng Hall, Blackberry Lane, Coventry CV2 3JS (01203 638660).

Jet Publications, 67 Musters Road, Ruddington, Nottingham NG11 6JB (0115 984 5960).

7

Supporting Parents with Younger Children

▌It takes a whole village to raise a child (quoted in Ball 1994).

In this chapter we consider how we can make appropriate provision for parents with babies and toddlers in early childhood settings. We describe how to set up a suitably challenging and secure environment for children under three and how best to provide for parents with very different needs and expectations.

Most early years workers responsible for admissions policies in education and care settings are very aware of the huge unmet need for places for children under three years. Far more women are now returning to work whilst their children are under statutory school age. In the late 1990s there has been a huge increase in demand from parents for a range of education and day care services. Forty-six per cent of women with children under five years now work. Because there has been no national childcare policy in the UK many parents have struggled to find what they need within the public, private and voluntary sectors. Parents have had to place their very young children in a wide range of settings – workplace crèches, social services day nurseries, private day nurseries, in playgroups, with childminders or with relations.

In some of these settings the early years experiences offered to children are of high quality. The Children Act 1989 now sets some minimum standards for quality care. Parents are however very aware that quality varies considerably between settings. Parents often express a preference for provision where there is an educational focus, but very few nursery schools or nursery classes offer places to children under three. Nor do they offer children the kind of hours that might support working parents. With a new government and a national policy (Early Excellence, 1996) for children under five we may yet see the development of high quality education and care centres. These would be more responsive to the hours that parents work and would offer high quality education and care to meet the needs of children below three years and from three to five years.

A large number of women and some men are not employed outside the home and will spend long periods of time with their young children. Britain has the largest level of lone-parent families in Europe, so an increasing number of parents are bringing up their children without the support of a partner. Many of these families are living on low incomes since poverty has increased significantly in the last twenty years (poverty affects one in three children today). Other parents combine bringing up their young families with work outside the home.

Parents' needs for adult contact and shared care

Consider the needs that these parents might have:

Colette and Jim share bringing up their children and both go out to work. Jim works a continental shift which alternates between 6.00 am to 2.00 pm, 2.00 pm to 10.00 pm and 10.00 pm to 6.00 am. Colette is working a regular 2.00 pm to 10.00 pm shift. This means that sometimes they need extended child care and other times they hand over their two year old in the entrance to the factory where they both work. Both Colette and Jim are very committed to their children's education but they also want to make sure that they have a nice home, a garden for the children to play in, holidays, days out, toys and treats.

Siobhan and her partner combine bringing up a young family with their work commitments in a very different way. Siobhan's partner works fairly traditional hours, from 8.30 am – 4.30 pm. Siobhan takes the older children to school and then goes to her job as a playgroup supervisor three mornings a week. Her youngest child (a two year old) can stay with her in the playgroup. At 3.15 pm she collects her two older children from school, and cooks them tea. When her partner arrives home she goes out to her evening job, as a foreman in a factory, from 5.00 pm – 10.00 pm. Siobhan's partner, Colin, looks after the children from teatime until Siobhan comes home. He likes to help the older children with their homework and walks them up the road to an after-school club once a week. He finds his two year old fairly demanding after a full day's work and he often wonders if he's 'getting it right' for her.

Jamila is 18 and a lone parent. She has two young children under three years who have no contact with their father. She is at home alone with the children all day and often feels very isolated in the evenings. She works at the weekend and earns just a little more than she would get if she stayed on benefit. During the week her mum and dad are working, but at the weekend they look after their grandchildren. If Jamila left her children with a registered childminder she could claim an allowance for childcare, but she thinks they are too young to be left with someone outside the family. Jamila enjoys going to work for the social life and because it makes her feel like she can still do some of the things she used to do before she had the children. Her youngest child has special educational needs and she spends many hours each week going to clinics and keeping appointments with health professionals.

Kayleigh is a young parent with twin daughters six months old, and a three year old. She lives in a small village where there is no nursery school, although there is a small playgroup attached to the local primary school. Kayleigh was very depressed after the birth of her first child and spent some time as an inpatient in a psychiatric unit for mothers and babies. After the birth of the twins she became increasingly isolated and found it very hard to respond to her children's needs. Her partner was recently made redundant and now has to work as a sales rep and is away from home at least two nights a week.

It should be clear from these examples that while some parents will need extended daycare and education provision for their children, many others want something different. A range of services are needed during the day and sometimes in the early evening, where parents can get some of the following:

> ▶ practical support in a welcoming environment
> ▶ companionship, a chance to meet other parents and some time for themselves
> ▶ a stimulating play experience for their baby or toddler and a chance to share the care.

Many parents feel very isolated whilst they are bringing up their children and their self-esteem is often at its lowest ebb at this time. Bringing up a young family can make it hard for parents to achieve any kind of balance in their life. The demands of children and housework, and the need to earn a living or support a partner are unremitting. Men and women who are bringing up children on their own or who are the primary carer on a daily basis often experience a loss of identity. This kind of loneliness, tiredness and self-doubt can sometimes lead to depression.

Most parents love their children and want the best for them. They know only too well that the first years of a child's life are very important. Some parents may even have attended courses on 'parenting skills' during their last years at school. All new parents receive messages from health and education professionals, friends and family about how parenting 'should' be done. They are presented with a very strong and often romanticised media image of what family life should be like, and how good parents ought to behave. Life with a young baby or toddler rarely bears any resemblance to how it's portrayed in the media. Sometimes parents find it hard to enjoy their babies and toddlers and then feel let down and very guilty. They may be feeling isolated and depressed, or just overwhelmed with the responsibilities of bringing up a family. Many parents with young children experience severe financial hardship and this makes it difficult for them to see a future when they won't be so tired or so anxious about getting things right. Parents are often faced with difficult choices: buying disposable nappies or something to eat. The demands of mortgages and the stress of busy work schedules all add to parental stress. Men in the UK work longer hours than in any other European country and this results in added responsibility and pressure for women at home and alone most of the time.

Babies and toddlers need the important adults in their lives, particularly their primary care givers, to be very much in tune with how they are feeling and what they are thinking. From birth, babies build up an emotional rapport with their care givers and begin to establish a dialogue with them. If their parent or care giver is over anxious, preoccupied with other things, or withdrawn and depressed, it makes it very difficult for this special relationship to develop fully. Researchers have found that children who don't have a stimulating environment, who aren't encouraged to play and are rarely touched have brains that are much less well developed.

Surveys were carried out in several local authorities to find out just what kind of additional services parents wanted for children under four and for children aged three to five years. Researchers were surprised to find that often full-time day care was **not** top of parents' agenda. Parents were much

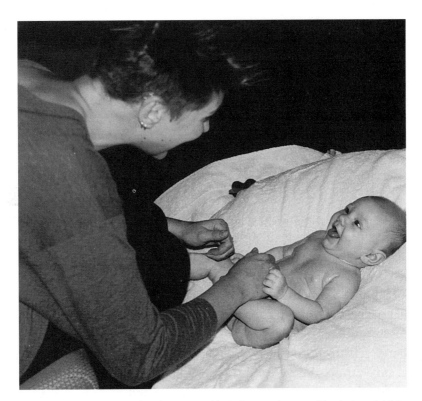

From birth, babies build up an emotional rapport with their care givers, and begin to establish a dialogue with them

more interested in shared care and support in their role as their child's first educator and primary care giver. When asked, the parents said that what they wanted was somewhere to go to, often for quite short periods of time. They wanted to be able to share their anxieties and meet and talk to other parents including parents with older children. They wanted a warm and welcoming setting. They wanted advice from professionals about the kinds of materials and experiences they could offer their young children. Parents also wanted to be in a setting where their children could play happily and safely and where their learning was supported and extended.

Children's rights – security and stimulation

Babies and children under three need to feel secure and special and need to spend a lot of their time with the people that are most important to them. The important adults in a child's life could be the child's biological parents, foster parents or step-parents, their grandparents, close family friends, childminders or their key worker in a nursery or playgroup setting.

Babies and toddlers also need to spend time with other children and they need lots of stimulation. Elinor Goldschmied has made some wonderful videos of babies and toddlers playing with exciting natural materials and with each other. She points out how important it is for early workers to make a suitably challenging provision for children under three (Goldschmied and Jackson, 1991). Her video material also shows how very young children benefit from gazing, touching, stroking and playing with each other and with well-chosen materials, whilst the important adults in their lives stay close by.

In many countries, it would be seen as unusual for babies and toddlers to spend long periods of time within the family home with the exclusive attention of one parent. Babies and toddlers up to three years are often carried around and held close to their parent's body. In these countries children spend their time in a variety of environments and meet many different adults and children during the hours that they are awake.

In Northern Italy in the town of Emilia Romagna there are high quality education and care services for children under four years. Parents and early years workers feel that children are being deprived if they don't spend at least some of their time with their young friends in the town's well-equipped nurseries. In Italian nurseries they believe it is important even for very young children to begin to care for each other.

In a day care setting in Milan staff and parents from a British nursery centre saw how this peer group support can work in practice. Two toddlers climbed into a tunnel from opposite ends and got stuck in the middle and began to cry and call out in great distress. Staff rushed to their aid and so did the whole nursery cohort! When the toddlers were safe once more, they were patted and petted by their nursery friends. Even though most of the communication was non-verbal they were clearly giving each other a lot of emotional support. One British visitor ruefully noted, 'In our nursery I think the other children would just have laughed at their distress.'

As early years educators in the UK we need to be aware that there is not one 'right' way of bringing up children and that we have a lot to learn from other countries and different cultures. Clearly the special bond between baby or toddler and their primary care givers is important but babies and toddlers do also benefit from the company of their peers.

Educational provision for babies and toddlers

Babies and toddlers need the company of other children and supportive, responsive adults. They also have the right to a high quality developmentally appropriate educational provision. Traditionally early years workers in the UK have focused on one of two things:

> ▶ early years education for the three to fives
> ▶ care for the under threes.

This way of working has been challenged by researchers and practitioners. We now know that children from three to five years need stimulation, intellectual challenge and adults who can support and extend their learning. They also need a key worker or special person who is familiar to them, understands their behaviour, is friendly with their family and knows their home background. Children in nursery schools, nursery centres, day nurseries or playgroups aren't able to engage in deep level learning unless they have high self-esteem and a sense of self-efficacy. They need to know that they are loved and lovable and that the important adults in their lives see them as capable and competent.

A child whose well-being is high will feel like a fish in water (Laevers, 1995).

Babies and toddlers also need a stimulating play environment, and playful, demanding adults who are willing to interact with them. They need lots of cuddles and positive touch from adults who aren't afraid of intimate relationships. They need adults who are clear and able to set appropriate boundaries with them.

You should not make too many assumptions about what is good for young children. Not all babies and toddlers want to be comforted in the same way. Some children may want to be rocked and held when they have hurt themselves or when they feel sad. Other children might prefer less physical contact and enjoy a gentle stroke or the sound of a reassuring familiar voice. Some toddlers need to rest between one exciting experience and the next; others are insatiable and can keep going all day. A suitable learning

Enjoying messy play

environment for babies and toddlers would need to include at least some of the following:

> ▶ clay for moulding, rolling ...
> ▶ sand for sieving, building . . .
> ▶ water for splashing, trickling, spraying, filling, emptying, flooding . . .
> ▶ peat for digging, making mounds, burying things . . .
> ▶ glue for sticking, spreading . . .
> ▶ paint, crayons, felt tips for self-expression
> ▶ treasure baskets full of natural materials and household objects for sensory explorations
> ▶ mirrors to reflect their own image, in bathrooms, playrooms
> ▶ opportunities for music and dance
> ▶ a space in which to run safely
> ▶ climbing and sliding equipment
> ▶ a bouncy space for jumping and diving
> ▶ a place where they can curl up, rest and relax
> ▶ dens and places to hide away from adults
> ▶ some personal space where they can develop their play without interruption from older siblings or adults.

Parents' different needs

Parents, like their babies and toddlers, have different needs and wants. It is important for staff to be clear about their own roles if we are to make suitable provision for parents in early years setting. Whilst most parents would welcome some practical support and the chance to share the care of their very young children, they would probably not want to see staff setting themselves up as parent substitutes. Parents may well ask for advice and be hungry for information on their children's health and development but they would also need staff to acknowledge their critical role as their child's first educator.

Making your setting accessible

Most parents with babies and toddlers would welcome and benefit from the kind of provision that we've described. If it was to be equally accessible to all parents it would need to be locally based and a free service. In fact, many nursery schools, day nurseries and playgroups where their provision is primarily focused on children from aged three to five are already offering groups and drop-in facilities to parents with younger children. However, not all parents will find it easy to access these services for their under threes. Think about the obstacles that might stand in the way of the parents in these case studies.

Malika is Bengali and was born in Calcutta. She married and moved to small town in the Midlands where there were no other Bengali families. On the estate where she lives there are no other families from a minority ethnic group. Her daughter has been at primary school for six months now and her two year old son is very bored at home without his sister. She knows that the school has a parent craft group where parents and toddlers are welcome but she's not sure when they meet or who leads the group and finds it hard to go and ask.

Barry is in his early 40s and is a single parent with two children. One already goes to the nursery centre but the youngest is still at home. Barry used to be a middle manager in a small company but gave up his job when his wife left him with custody of the children. He and his young family currently live in a hostel and if he is to achieve the number of points required to boost him up the housing list he needs to keep his room and shared living area very neat and tidy. He has to take his youngest son out with him for most of the day. He knows that there is a mother and toddler messy play session at the nursery centre where his eldest daughter goes each day but he feels that as the only man he wouldn't be welcome.

Connie lives in an estate which is a long walk or bus ride from the nearest playgroup which takes children aged from three years. She has five girls under the age of seven. Her partner drops the eldest two off at their primary school on his way to work. Connie has to take a double buggy wherever she goes and is always worried about losing track of her three year old who is into everything. She feels that she has no time at all for the youngest child, a baby of seven months. Connie finds it hard even to get to the baby clinic which is held in the local church hall. She tried to register her three year old for the playgroup but couldn't get her there regularly and she didn't settle.

If we are going to offer services in our early childhood settings for parents with their babies and toddlers then we will need to think hard about ensuring the services are really accessible to parents like Connie, Barry and Malika. These are some of the questions you might need to consider.

> ▶ How are services advertised?
> ▶ Is knowledge about the services readily available or dependent on word of mouth?
> ▶ Do the other professionals who regularly visit families at home (for example, health visitors) know about the service?
> ▶ Is publicity material visually attractive and published in several languages and circulated in several different places such as health centres, churches, shops and local factories?
> ▶ Are services run at times that suit parents and very young children (for example, some toddlers sleep in the afternoon and may need a morning session)?
> ▶ Are crèche facilities available for toddlers so that parents can give their babies some special time?
> ▶ Are services 'men friendly'?
> ▶ Are they accessible to parents and children with disabilities?
> ▶ Is the environment warm and welcoming and is there someone available to pick up on parents' needs? Is the play provision suitable for both babies and toddlers? Are there facilities for changing babies?

There are different kinds of provision for babies and toddlers that might be set up in early years settings such as day nurseries, family centres, nursery schools/classes or playgroups, and here are some examples.

Setting up a baby clinic

Baby clinics run by regional health authorities are available all over the country and are offered in diverse settings. They may be in health centres, in church halls or nurseries. Almost all new parents use a baby clinic for at least the first few months after their child is born. It is a service that parents can use without being labelled in any way. When baby clinics work well there is generally a health visitor available for parents to talk to, who can give professional advice and personal support to parents. Babies are weighed and their development is monitored.

In many early childhood settings it should be possible to set up a space and make it available for the health authority to use for a local clinic. What your setting has to offer the health authority is that it is a familiar, attractive, comfortable and easily accessible space for local parents. A baby clinic should ideally be set up so that there is:

> ▶ a warm quiet area where individual parents can talk confidentially to a health visitor and weigh their baby
> ▶ comfortable adult chairs arranged in a semi-circle with bean bags or bouncy chairs provided for the younger children
> ▶ treasure baskets full of interesting household objects which babies can play with safely
> ▶ a volunteer worker available to make coffee and tea for parents who may have walked some distance
> ▶ leaflets and interesting materials about local services and resources
> ▶ a play worker available to play alongside the toddlers.

One nursery centre which invited the local health authority to set up a baby clinic found that the particular staff assigned by the local authority made a lot of difference to the parents. In the beginning the baby clinic was set up very formally with a table and scales at the front and hard backed chairs set up in rows. There was no tea or coffee or play equipment available. First-time parents found it hard to talk to each other or to the health visitor in this schoolroom atmosphere. After a few months a new health visitor was assigned to the clinic and it was set up as much like a domestic sitting room as possible, although clearly care had to be taken regarding health and safety

Baby clinics can be held in attractive, comfortable and easily accessible early year settings. They need to be for local parents

issues. A volunteer came in to make coffee and to make sure cups were always kept out of the way of the children. Play experiences were set up within the circle of chairs and another volunteer was introduced to play with and support the slightly older children. A corner of the room was set aside for the digital scales where parents and health visitors could chat. Almost overnight the numbers using the clinic increased. Some of these parents already had children in the nursery. Many more became interested in what was going on there and filled in application forms for the future. Fathers who used to simply drop their partners off began to feel okay about coming into the clinic room. Often parents using the clinic spent the whole afternoon there sharing ideas and getting feedback on their children's development and welfare (parents were interested in topics such as breastfeeding versus bottle feeding and whether to allow their baby to have injections or not).

A member of the nursery staff talked to Carole about how she felt about the clinic.

Carole has used the nursery on and off for twelve years. Her son Craig who is now fourteen years old came when he was eighteen months old with Carole to the baby clinic on her health visitor's advice. Carole now has a six month old daughter and once again regularly attends the baby clinic. She enjoys the informal way the clinic is run. The baby clinic nearer to her house is very formal and she feels there is no time for her to talk about any worries as the staff are always very busy. At the nursery baby clinic she can sit and have a coffee and a chat. If she wants to get Lara weighed she can. Some weeks she chooses not to, but enjoys talking to the other women who use the clinic. Carole feels it is a good excuse for her to escape the four walls at home and find some company and support.

Aromatherapy and baby massage sessions

Aromatherapy involves the use of special essential oils which are extracted from plants. Many are beneficial to health and can be used in massage. Many parents find it hard to know how much they should touch, cuddle or hold their children. The message from manufacturers of baby care equipment is – not a lot! Children in this country are strapped and carried in large plastic containers, put into cots behind bars, wheeled in buggies and see the world through a transparent wind and rain protection shield. When they are awake often they are hung between doorways in bouncy harnesses or put into the middle of large plastic walkers.

Some parents worry that if they rock, hold and comfort their babies too much then they will never settle with anyone else. Some fathers report that they are afraid to stroke or touch their babies because of media messages about child sexual abuse. Parents **need** to experience holding, touching and rocking their children. Babies are all different, and bottle fed and breast fed babies like to be held in very different ways. Whilst holding babies close and touching and massaging them is seen as very natural in many cultures, parents in the UK almost need permission to touch, smell and massage their naked baby. Increasingly, early years workers are setting up aromatherapy and baby massage sessions to encourage parents to enjoy touching and cuddling their children.

Running an aromatherapy session in an early childhood setting can be extremely rewarding. Here a parent and voluntary worker describe how a group was set up:

Parents were showing a lot of interest in aromatherapy and massage, and the oils were freely available for people to buy in high street and smaller chemists. Many of our parents were a bit unsure about what it was alright to use and how much they should use on very young children.

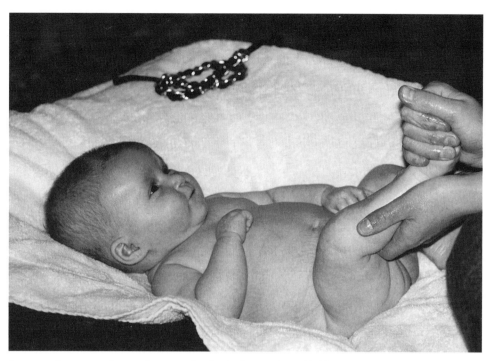

An aromatherapy session can be rewarding for both parents and babies

Jill, the health visitor, did a ten-week introductory basic course in aromatherapy and massage at the local college. This gave us some basic knowledge about this subject. Then we went on to design posters and spread the word to other health visitors and in general in the town about what we were offering at this group through the centre.

The response from parents was immediate and today we have a 16–26 strong group of parents regularly using our sessions, paying 20 pence towards costs.

We now have a qualified massage and aromatherapist whom we use for training and advice. She is available for questions at any time. She also supplies all we need in base oils at an extremely reasonable price. After six years we now have two aromatherapy sessions a week, one on a Monday afternoon which is smaller and more intimate and run by parent volunteers and a health visitor. The Thursday morning session is a larger group and takes three voluntary members, at least, to organise and run, including a health visitor.

Aromatherapy and baby massage sessions can be run in any early childhood setting where there is a warm, friendly, carpeted room and enthusiastic staff who are willing to do at least the basic ten-week course at a local Further Education College. It is, however, critical to have professional health visitor involvement at least in an advisory capacity. The parents who attend these sessions often have serious anxieties about their children, and worries about their own feelings that are health-related. Specialist advice is also needed because it is very important that aromatherapy essential oils are used in the correct way. For instance, they must be diluted in 'carrier' oils. Concentrated oils can be harmful to adults and children. Some oils should not be used with children at all.

Volunteers and health visitors running aromatherapy and baby massage sessions find that some parents walk in through the door having heard about the sessions. Other parents may be referred to the session by GPs, health visitors or voluntary organisations like Home Start because they have experienced post-natal depression. One such parent whose husband died when their baby was born could hardly touch her child at all. At first a friend came with her to the baby massage session. The friend brought the baby into the group whilst the mum sat outside. After about four weeks she felt able to come into the room and gradually found it possible to touch and be intimate with her baby. Generally such parents need a lot of very gentle support.

Generally aromatherapy and baby massage sessions need to be structured so that the following are in place.

> ▶ There is a warm, friendly quiet room with gentle music in the background.
> ▶ There is a circle of comfortable adult chairs with beanbags or cushions in the middle and fresh towels for each child.
> ▶ Parents make their own decisions about how much skin-to-skin touch they feel comfortable with. They choose the oils from a selection carefully selected by the health visitor and trained volunteer as appropriate to the age range of children attending.
> ▶ There are treasure baskets available for younger toddlers to explore and crèche facilities or nursery places for older siblings so that the babies can get the attention they need.
> ▶ There needs to be a set number of parents and children attending each session so that real relationships can be established.

The kinds of conversations that parents have with staff and volunteers whilst their babies are enjoying this intimate and appropriate touch can be very deep. Conventional boundaries seem to break down more easily whilst everyone is preoccupied with engaging in physical contact with their baby. Parents feel able to talk about bleeding after pregnancy, how yucky their child's tummy button looks or how worried they are about tiny blue bruises or birthmarks on their baby's back.

Parents attending these aromatherapy and baby massage sessions are spending time **tuning into their children**. As well as making intimate physical contact with their babies and toddlers in a whole new way they are also gazing intently at them, talking to them, singing to them, reassuring them with language as well as touch. Neuroscientists say that 'repeated experience' is what 'wires up' a child's brain. Clearly aromatherapy and baby massage is just the sort of experience that can lead to a stronger relationship between parent and child, and a healthier child.

A nursery worker talked to Sue, who is 30 years old and has three children, Luke, seven years, Sophie, four years and Joshua thirteen weeks, about what she got out of going to the aromatherapy session in her local early years centre.

First time around Sue was using the playgroup for her eldest son Luke and while settling him in she waited in the family room, where she met Kay, the health visitor, who co-led the aromatherapy group. Kay encouraged her to attend the massage session and introduced her to the other mums.

The second time Sue knew the times the massage sessions ran and came along, having previously booked a place for Sophie who needed the crèche. Joshua was only a few weeks old and was suffering from very bad jaundice and Sue wanted to spend some time with him without the demands of the other children. Sue told the group she has been diagnosed as having post-natal depression. Coming to baby massage seemed her only legitimate way out of the house. Sometimes she said she forced herself to come to the massage group, knowing that once she got there her whole day felt easier to cope with. She found talking to the other women gave her a lot of support.

She spoke of how important it was to be around other people when she was feeling so low. She described how her days all used to blur into one another but were slowly beginning to separate out into good days and bad days.

Other groups for parents and toddlers

EARLY DAZE (FOR BABIES UP TO ONE YEAR)

Many parents feel in a 'daze' after their baby is born especially if they have toddlers and school-aged children to cope with as well. It can be easy to become trapped into a routine of housework, food shopping, taking and collecting children from school with little time for yourself or for the new baby.

However, not all parents want, or are ready for, the kind of physical contact that goes on in the aromatherapy and baby massage group. They simply want a place to come to that is warm and friendly where they can have a break, a chat and also keep their babies happy and 'amused'.

This kind of group could be set up in the corner of a hall, in a staffroom in an early years setting or a classroom as long as the setting can provide:

> ▶ reasonably comfortable adult-sized chairs
> ▶ a soft carpet and cushions for the babies, and treasure baskets
> ▶ appropriate play provision for the toddlers
> ▶ tea- and coffee-making facilities
> ▶ a group leader – often an experienced parent and/or an early childhood educator (preferably with some training in active listening or counselling skills).

Parents comment that these sorts of groups tend to bring the 'playground' chat inside the nursery. Parents exchange birth stories, discuss important decisions that they have to make, about breast feeding or bottle feeding, or about vaccinations, and gain supportive friendship. Perhaps most important of all, they watch how other parents behave with their children.

FIRST STEPS

Once toddlers are walking fairly freely they are ready for a different kind of play experience. It may be quite hard to wean parents and children from a group they have been attending regularly for a year but for the sake of new babies coming into the baby clinic, aromatherapy group and Early Daze groups it will be important for you to move on to a setting which offers some facilities for parents with toddlers on the move.

The layout of the room needs to change for this kind of group (see figure 7.1). The children are making their first tentative steps away from their

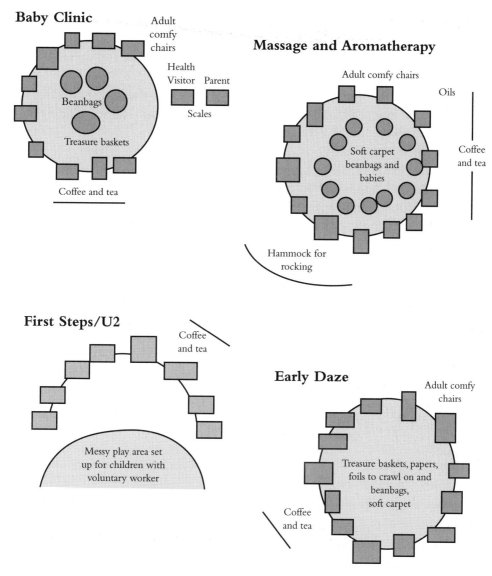

Figure 7.1 Room layout is critical. Different groups have different needs

parents or primary care givers and they need some space. The adult chairs need to be set up in a semi-circle so that parents can watch, get up and get involved, and also respect their toddlers need to take a few risks. These groups are often attended by childminders as well as parents. One local childminder who was looking after up to seven different children during the average week told the group leader of the parent and toddler group she attended, 'I'd go mad if I had to stay at home all day. I couldn't childmind and be on my own all the time.'

Toddler groups need to offer parents and children:

> ▶ a warm, safe and welcoming environment with tea and coffee
> available and comfy adult chairs
> ▶ the kind of 'messy play' provision for toddlers that most parents
> would feel reluctant to set up at home on a daily basis including
> sand, water, peat, clay, paint
> ▶ if 'messy play' is impossible or impractical because of the
> constraints of the space or because parents don't want it, there
> needs to be a well thought out alternative provision that is
> developmentally appropriate. For example, building bricks, hollow
> blocks, dens and dressing-up clothes, pots, pans and household
> materials as well as more traditional materials like stickle bricks,
> felt tips and paper
> ▶ the chance to chat about serious social issues, with speakers
> invited to speak on topics such as first aid for children.

Parents report that what they gain most from coming to such groups is the chance to check out that the way they are handling their children is appropriate. 'Is it okay to smack your child? Is it safe to smack your child?' 'How can you set your boundaries if you don't smack?' 'If your child bites or punches is he aggressive?' 'If your child won't share is she being selfish?'

A leader of a parent and toddler group in the local children's centre talked to Kate, a grandmother looking after her grandchild full-time, about how important the group was to her:

Kate is the grandmother of Bobby who is twenty months old. They both attend First Steps every week. This is a group specially geared up for parents with children between one and two years. The co-leaders of the group are aware that Bobby needs extra attention because he has been hitting and hurting other children. Kate is aware that Bobby needs to interact with other children. Bobby's mum works full-time and is a single parent and Kate and Bobby's grandad James care for him full-time. Often Kate feels she has to leave with Bobby half-way through a session because of his behaviour. Recently she stayed away two weeks to give Bobby, herself and the whole group a break from each other as it was too much for her to deal with.

The co-leaders of the group are working with Kate and Bobby as much as they can. Kate needs lots of reassurance and practical strategies for coping with Bobby. The group is set up to offer play experiences that stimulate children, where children can begin to learn how to share, take turns and develop their own ways of relating to other children.

Sandra explained how she feels about the Baby Massage and Early Daze groups.

My name is Sandra and I've got two children. Emma, she's eight months old and Aimee, she's also eight months old – they're twins.

I go to the Baby Massage once a week normally on a Monday afternoon and I go to Early Daze on a Thursday afternoon. I find that the Baby Massage is really interesting and it really helps the twins a lot – it really seems to settle them, and I find it interesting as well. It's something unusual, something different and it's somewhere to go, somewhere to mix. Everybody's really friendly there. Also with the Early Daze group everyone is really helpful and dead friendly. I seem to get on well with everybody. Nobody sort of pesters you, they just let you get on with it, which is really what I like. I've been going to Baby Massage for a few months now. I think the twins enjoy it. I'm not sure, but I think it sends them to sleep which is what it's supposed to do. Early Daze is not like some groups I've been to. I've used a couple of groups where they're too into your business and want to know everything, but with Early Daze and Baby Massage you sort of come and go as you please, there are no sort of questions asked or anything like that. I like the people that work there especially Karen and Carol (parent volunteers) – they're not like workers they're just like another person really. They treat you like a human being which is good.

I'll probably carry on using groups when the twins are older because I find it really helpful. The groups have really brought my confidence out because I was really shy at first. I sort of stand up now and say what I think whereas before I wouldn't!

Summary

▶ Babies and toddlers need to develop relationships with their peers and with the adults they come into contact with. This means that the same staff should regularly run these sessions. It also means that the number of children in each session needs to be limited so that real peer friendships can be formed.

▶ There are real benefits for parents who have this kind of support and can share the care of their young children with other parents, volunteers and early childhood educators in early years settings. Parents generally become more relaxed about their parenting and have more to give to their children emotionally. They understand and cater for their child's developmental needs more effectively and feel better about themselves.

▶ Parents are not a homogeneous group. Early childhood settings need to offer, if possible, a number of different kinds of groups for parents with babies and toddlers. Some parents will reject aromatherapy and massage and hate 'messy play' but would come into sessions which are less child-centred, for example, discussion groups. These would be equally valuable to them and to their children if there is appropriate play provision or a crèche.

▶ Some parents may want and need to go from one group to another. This doesn't mean that they've become 'group dependent'. It is not an unhealthy dependency – they haven't become 'groupies'. As the children grow their needs change, and parents will want to be able to access different kinds of experiences for them.

▶ Most early childhood settings don't have enough staff to offer these kinds of services without support from volunteers or other agencies. It's very important to network with other professionals like Child & Family Guidance, Health Visitors and others and to offer parents training and encourage them to become group leaders. There are also national organisations such as Community Service Volunteers who will place students in early childhood settings.

▶ Groups don't suit everybody. Some parents may prefer to continue to meet the friends they have made through ante-natal classes in their own home or in other settings. Some parents may find it just too hard to come into a group setting. They may want to talk to someone individually about childcare issues, their own health issues or their mixed feelings about being a parent.

Bibliography

Ball, C., (1994) Start Right: The Importance of Early Learning. London: Royal Society of Arts.

Carob, A., (1987) Working with Depressed Women: A Feminist Approach. London: Gower.

Department of Health, (1991) The Children Act 1989. Family Support Day Care and Educational Provision for Young Children Vol. 2. London: HMSO.

Goldschmied, E. and Jackson, S., (1991) People under 3 – Quality in day care. London: Routledge.

Early Excellence, (1996). London: Labour Party.

Laevers, F., (1995) Lecture at Worcester College of Higher Education.

Nash, J.M., (1992) Fertile Minds. Article in *Time* 3rd February. p. 35–42.

Rouse Selleck, D. (ed), (1990) Babies and Toddlers: Carers and Educators Quality for the Under 3s. National Children's Bureau. All the papers in this report are well worth reading; particularly useful is P.A. Calder's 'Education Care Advantage to Under threes'.

White, M., (1992) A review of the Influence and Effects of Portage in Wolfendale, S., Working with Parents of SEN Children After the Code of Practice. London: David Fulton.

Useful videos

Goldschmied, E., (1987) Infants at Work (training video). Available from the early childhood unit. London: National Children's Bureau.

Goldschmied, E. and Hughes, A., (1994) Heuristic Play with Objects (training video). London: National Children's Bureau.

Goldschmied, E. and Selleck, D., (1996) Communication between Babies in the First Year (video and training guide). London: National Children's Bureau.

8

Support for Families who have Children with Special Educational Needs

Parents can be effective only if professionals take notice of what they say and how they express their needs and treat their contributions as intrinsically important (Warnock Report, 1978).

This chapter addresses what it is like to be part of a family where there is a child with special educational needs. It also looks at how early years professionals fit in and what their role might be.

Issues change all the time for families who have children with special educational needs. When a child with a disability is born the response from parents is complicated. Parents have to come to terms with their sorrow as well as celebrating a new birth. Often parents do not know the nature of their child's disability at birth. They may spend many months, sometimes even years, fighting for a formal assessment of their child's emotional or physical needs.

Throughout this process families suffer enormous amounts of tension and stress. Siblings born before or after the child with special needs can experience real difficulties. Parents can be very anxious for them to achieve. Sometimes families are simply overwhelmed by the amount of emotional and physical energy they need to give to the child with special educational needs.

Over time parents learn to accept and adapt. Their child grows and hopefully receives appropriate care and resources. He or she attends school, gets involved, makes friends. However, as their child matures the family has to contend with puberty and growing up. Young adults with special educational needs may find leaving home particularly difficult and parents may find letting go doubly hard. These parents have to cope with many difficult days and often develop an enormous amount of personal strength.

What is a disability or special educational need?

The term 'special needs' is now being used for many children. Not only does it often cover children who may be struggling with their reading or writing skills, but it is often used as a label for children who have a physical or visual disability. We all have special needs of one kind or another. At different times in our lives we require help, either physically or mentally. For example, most of us have to use a dictionary for our spelling – we have to find the resources to help ourselves! It is important to be aware of our own struggles when working with children and adults who have any kind of a disability.

Children with physical disabilities may well have long-term requirements to enable them to grow to their full potential. Children may need to be measured regularly so that their 'special' wheelchair or standing frame 'grows' with them. Not all schools are able to cater for children with disabilities. Parents may have to find out where the specially designated provisions are within their local authority. If necessary they may have to ask for transport to use these facilities.

Children who have learning difficulties may also need specialised long-term support. In many cases making an assessment of these children's special needs is a complex process. It can be a long time before a clear diagnosis can be made of their condition.

There are also children who need short-term support for their language development or to help them with their reading skills. These children's needs can often be met through mainstream schooling. They will however require regular assessment from a teacher with specialised skills together with parents and other professionals. Children themselves should be consulted when making these arrangements.

Even if children have the same disabilities they are still individuals and feel different to one another. It's important to remember this when working with them and their parents.

How early years professionals might get involved

Finding the families

The needs of a three year old with a disability living with his or her family are very different to those of a twenty year old with a disability who may wish for some independence and a place to call his or her own. The age of the child or young person you are working with will very much alter the way you get involved.

As an early years professional you may work within the family, perhaps as a nanny for a child with special educational needs – in which case you would become very much part of the child's life and daily routine. You would have an important role to play at mealtimes and bedtimes.

As a support worker in a playgroup, nursery school or primary school you might only see the children for around ten hours a week. Whatever part you are playing, knowing and recognising the child as an individual is of utmost importance. All children with special educational needs are **people** first. **They should not be defined by their disability.** It is so easy to damage the self-esteem of any child, but this is particularly true of any child with disabilities. We can do this by jumping in too soon and taking over and making things too easy for them. Just think for a moment: if there is something you have just learned to manage alone and now someone does it for you – how do you feel?

Whether you are working in the home or another setting your role as an early childhood educator is to make it possible for children with special educational needs to experience an inclusive education. They need to have equal access to all the learning experiences on offer. **Children with special educational needs need to have a chance to 'have a go'.**

When you are working with a child with special educational needs you often find yourself working with other agencies. Most children with any kind of disability have many caring adults involved in their lives, from physiotherapists to taxi drivers. Your role will be to work with and fit around others who are offering a professional service to the child in your care.

Sometimes there are too many professionals and services involved and you may have to help parents identify who or what is most useful to them.

Meeting the families

Many nurseries, early years centres and reception classes now home visit families and this is especially important if parents have children with special educational needs and no access to transport. Walking into a new environment such as a nursery class may be too difficult for many parents. If parents are not on the phone it is important to write to make contact and arrange a home visit that suits them. When making a home visit it is very important to listen to the family and what they are asking for. It may not be what you think they need!

We often make the assumption that families with children with special educational needs need a break from the child. In fact they often need a break from everything else in order that they can spend some special time with that child. Maybe what they really need is someone to help with practical tasks like the washing-up. It's worth finding out about local support groups and having their telephone numbers to hand. It will also be important to take something with you for the child to play with. That way parents may find it easier to focus on sharing their views with you.

An important lesson to learn is that you will never know everything that parents ask you. There is nothing wrong with not knowing, in fact it may help the parent/carer to believe that they themselves are the expert on their child. If you are prepared to sit and listen they will be able to tell you many new and different things about their child on every visit. It is important that you follow up a home visit with a phone call or a note confirming what you and the parents have agreed to do.

You may be the first professional visitor or the tenth professional visitor that the family has had that week. The family may also have felt let down many times by other professionals. It may be that parents would like to go to a support group but need your physical or emotional support to get them there. Going to new places and meeting new faces, having to 'tell their story', may just be too much to face alone. Sometimes when you do make a home visit it's just not the right time. Perhaps it's too soon and the parents have not yet been able to deal with or accept their child's special needs. There are also families for whom a home visit is too threatening. They may want to meet in a more formal setting.

It may take a long time to get to know the parents: one home visit is rarely enough to build a relationship. If you don't have time to make more than one visit, then maintaining a good relationship can be made easier by just dropping the parents a note or phoning them up now and again. Support groups and specialised knowledge are not always needed – often a friendly face and a chat is just as effective.

> Many professionals continue to suffer from 'parentitis' – a mixture of prejudice, ambivalence and ignorance of the strengths, concerns and insight of parents . . . one wonders whether one of the protracted and bloody battles that take place between agencies and individual parents . . . could have been avoided if professionals had behaved from the start with more empathy (Madden, 1995).

Starting off on the right foot

Keeping appointments may be difficult for a great number of reasons. The stresses on the family as a whole may be so high that remembering **who** they have to see and **when** can just be too much. As an early years professional meeting the family for the first time, the more adaptable you can be the better. When arranging to make a home visit ask the parents for a suitable time. Try not to make it sound like you are trying to give them yet another appointment. If the family is coming to meet you at your workplace have activities set up that are suitable for their child. Playdough and soft toys which make little noise are always useful, if you are trying to have a conversation. As you meet different children and their families you will also come across different medical conditions. Although the names of conditions have real significance parents find these labels very daunting. As an early childhood professional often you hear all about the child's condition before ever meeting the child and his or her family. Parents see the **child** first, not the condition and you need to do the same. Listen to the parents and whenever possible listen to the child. Between them they will tell you about their child's special needs and they will explain their struggles, their likes and dislikes.

No two families are ever the same. What some families find difficult others will find easy. The parents may not yet have accepted the medical diagnosis of their child's special needs. There may not be any formal diagnosis yet and they are simply trying to find out more about their child's condition.

Parents may be at different points in the grieving process. Some will have experienced giving birth to a child with special educational needs as 'losing the child they never had'. They have to come to terms with reality. Your role as an early childhood educator will be to help the family to celebrate their child's achievements and support him or her through the ups and downs of life.

Supporting siblings

Up to now we have spoken mainly about supporting the child with the disability and his or her parents. What happens if you are the brother or sister of a child with a disability? Depending on the age of the siblings the impact may be very different. Here are some examples of different children's reactions:

> ▶ 'My brother [with special educational needs] goes swimming every day. It's not fair.'
> ▶ My sister can write another language, not just in English' (a child boasting about her sister who has special educational needs).
> ▶ 'But I want us all to go out for the day. It's not my fault she's in that chair!'

Children with siblings who have special educational needs may well have completely different daily routines from their friends. They may experience name calling or bullying. They will often have questions that remain unanswered.

Children are very honest – they ask the questions they need to and, given appropriate explanations, they can often accept and understand difficult situations. There is often a lot of stigma attached to disabilities especially those where the child behaves in an 'unusual' way, perhaps in the middle of the supermarket or in the street. Adults often stare and find themselves unable to ask or offer help and children can sometimes be cruel.

This puts children with special educational needs and their siblings under a great deal of pressure. It may be that siblings experience unrealistic pressure and there is an assumption that they will always behave well and achieve highly. This may not be apparent when you first meet the family but it is always worth bearing in mind.

Grandparents also take on a different role when they have a grandchild with special educational needs. When grandchildren are born it is a time for celebration. Grandparents are generally supportive and offer advice and practical help when there is a new baby in the family. This can become difficult if the baby has a disability. Sometimes because of fear, anxiety and a feeling of not knowing how to help, grandparents take a back seat. This may leave the parents feeling very isolated. They often have no-one to talk to at a time when they really need support from people with whom they are intimate, such as close family. Visiting friends and family can sometimes be embarrassing, especially if their child has behavioural difficulties. Other family members can be judgmental and may assume that the child is badly behaved.

Going back to work for parents can be doubly difficult since their childcare needs may be very intensive. If they are working, not all work colleagues are equally supportive. Parents' self-esteem may well become low and relationships between parents often become stressful. Parents are faced with difficult questions: who do you look after first – yourself, your partner, your children? Whose needs come first? Families with children with special educational needs have to set up their own systems for survival. It is important to fit around them. In some families, extended family support may be very great, so they may not feel they need anyone else. However, if you are visiting parents who are confused and 'burnt out' you might decide that part of your role could be making a cup of tea or offering to play with one of the other children to give him or her some special time and attention. It is worth considering the possibility that the children or one or other partner may also need some extra help from other agencies.

Services for families with children with special educational needs

Parents who have children with special educational needs often have limited 'choices'. There are many groups and specialised services but the range of services will depend on where the family lives. Sometimes it seems that there are too many professionals involved in families. However, in rural areas there may be very few services available. The list below shows how many professionals a family may see regularly depending on the particular special educational needs their child experiences:

– doctor	– occupational therapist	– social worker
– consultant	– speech/language therapist	– support worker
– dentist	– support teacher	– taxi/transport driver
– physiotherapist	– suppliers of special equipment	– nurse

How much time does this leave for parents' friendships and social lives, or even for basic daily tasks? The disruption on the rest of the family is enormous. What happens to the brothers and sisters? Managing appointments alone can be a huge task especially if the parents don't have a car. The problem is that if the family says 'no' to any one of the professional supports that's offered they may appear unco-operative or uncaring. The following account and figure 8.1 show the journey one family had to take.

Hello, my name is Carole and I would like to share with you some of my experiences and views of the system during a ten-year period of my life.

I was married for five years when Siobhan was born. I had a very healthy pregnancy with no problems whatsoever (apart from the fact the doctors were unsure of my dates) until during the last few weeks when they said the baby was rather small and was not eating much, so the midwife started me off and Siobhan was born.

Like any new parents, we were so proud of our beautiful daughter, perfect in every way apart from her ears – they were folded flat forward but the paediatrician assured us they would correct themselves.

If only life was that simple.

At nine months old Siobhan saw the paediatrician who referred us to Oxford because he was concerned about the shape of her head. He said her skull had closed over too soon after birth and her development was not as it should be. As I was a new mother I was totally unaware at that time that there was any problem. How could I have been so naive?

When we got to Oxford we were sat down in front of about eight to ten different doctors, all from different departments, all looking for faults: the optician for her eyes, surgeon for her head and ears, physiotherapist, hip specialist, psychologist, even a psychiatrist. I was mortified to say the least. How dare they do this to us without any warning or consultation? It was like being thrown to the lions. I could perhaps have coped better if I had known what was wrong, but I didn't. Sadly, my husband was at a total loss as to what was happening – he assured me that everything would be okay, then left me to 'get on with it'.

Within weeks the appointments started to pile up. I recall my father saying to me, 'There's nothing wrong with her, she'll grow out of it.' Oh, how I wanted to scream at him. The next day was the final straw: an appointment with some top plastic surgeon came in the post. I sat on the stairs with a handful of appointments plus the one from the surgeon and I cried, 'You try telling

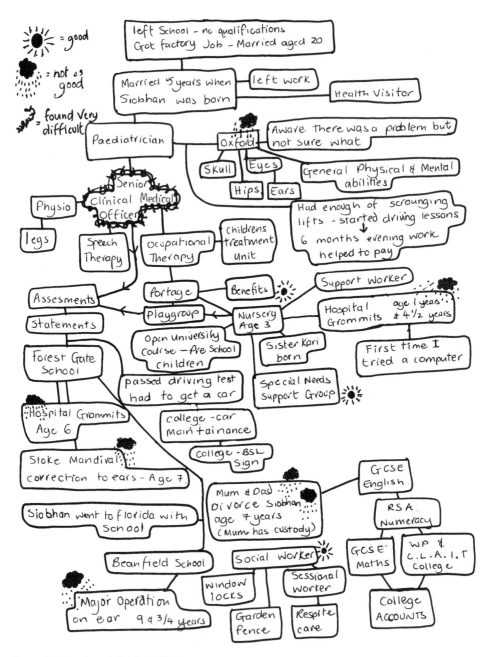

Figure 8.1 Carole and Siobhan's lifeline

me there was nothing wrong with my precious daughter.'

Strange as it may seem, that was the turning point. No point crying about

it: I had to be strong for Siobhan. So, mainly with my mother for support, I battled on into the future.

Over the next two years came physiotherapy, speech therapy, occupational therapy, portage*, visits to the children's treatment unit for group therapy (we had to attend these appointments every week for a couple of years). I worked evenings to pay for driving lessons as I could see I was going to need a car to keep up with everything! When Siobhan was two years old, I became pregnant with my second child.

I was working, keeping appointments and fitting in two driving lessons a week when I was pregnant. By this time my husband had very much taken a back seat and, with the ever-present help and support from my mother, I learned to thrive on my busy life. I enjoyed working, I needed it 'for me'. It was my only means of 'escape'. You can only take so much. I took two years of doctors and hospitals before I could crawl out from under them and say 'what about me?' without feeling guilty.

Once I had created a bit of space between me and 'them', I could see things much more clearly. I started to ask, 'Do we really need all this?' Too many people were doing the same job and, in all her innocence, I

think even Siobhan was getting confused by it all.

Siobhan had a cranial disorder (I think the word they used was 'cranialcystosus' or something to that effect). They thought because her skull had closed too soon that it was causing pressure on her brain and this was causing all her other problems. They took three years from Siobhan and me, three years of x-rays, photos, scans, tests and therapy to tell us they were sorry, but they could not find the root of the problem. There was no pressure on her brain and they could not tell me why she was the way she was. 'She is the way she is for no apparent reason,' was the best they could offer. There was no cure as she had no illness.

At the age of three Siobhan was able to attend the local nursery. With help and guidance from the nursery staff we were able to get support for Siobhan. By this time, my youngest daughter, Kari, had arrived. Most of the doctors and therapists were starting to back off now, and with Kari taking their place, I started to sink again. I joined the special needs support group at the nursery. This was an enormous help. I needed practical advice, how to cope with siblings, benefits I was entitled to, but most importantly how to enjoy 'time out' again.

Siobhan went through nursery and then on to a big school. Siobhan was

---

* Portage is a specialist service where trained workers home visit and support parents with children with special educational needs. Together, parents and portage workers devise a programme to encourage children and to help them develop basic skills.

'statemented' and it was decided she would go to a special school. I must admit that I was not happy with this. I felt in my heart that Siobhan was too advanced for this school and that it might in actual fact hold her back, but then again she was not advanced enough to go into mainstream school without support. She was stuck in 'no man's land'. I accepted the school and as it happened she got on very well. It was while she was there that my marriage finally broke down and we got a divorce.

Now how was I to get the help I really needed? The system is very good at offering you financial help, support and guidance, but what I needed now was an extra pair of hands, eyes in the back of my head and help to cope with my two children on my own.

This help came in the form of a social worker. I needed window locks to stop Siobhan climbing out of the windows, a new fence to stop her escaping. As she grew bigger, her needs changed and she became a lot more hard work. I needed a break. My social worker fought for two years to get me a fence and to eventually get respite care for Siobhan.

It is a struggle to maintain a good quality of life for Siobhan and, to me, this is where the system lets you down. There are things I need but the system will not provide them, like an extra pair of glasses for Siobhan (she is only entitled to one pair), cheap stabilisers for a big bike, an unbreakable video, a toilet and sink upstairs would be wonderful, a good computer would be great for her but alas, these sorts of things do not come in to it. They would make life so much easier.

After a couple of years her school closed down and all the children were moved to a 'Designated Special Provision' within a mainstream school. This was truly what I wanted for Siobhan and she is now thriving. Her school is at the opposite end of town from where I live. I passed my driving test and have a car. I need it if I am to attend the school for meetings, functions, collect Siobhan for appointments, etc. Running a car is a strain on the finances and I need it during the school holidays as Siobhan gets very bored. Because Siobhan can walk I am not entitled to mobility or a car. I don't need it to help her walk – I need it to maintain a quality of life for Siobhan, to stop her getting bored.

The system falls over itself to help with medical problems and care, but when it comes to quality of life they fall flat on their face. I have had to beg for help sometimes, not for me but for Siobhan. Is it so wrong of me to expect help? Siobhan did not ask to be born. I do my best under the circumstances but why should I not want better for my daughter?

Siobhan will soon be eleven and

Kari is eight. I have been a single parent for four years now. It has been a struggle but I can safely say we are a happy, content family now.

C. McIntyre

The statementing process

As an early childhood educator you may have to help parents who get involved in the statementing process. The statementing process can begin very early in a child's life, well before starting school. The length of time it takes to put a statement together should be no longer than six months. During this time any professional who has been or is involved in the child's well-being or education should submit a report stating any relevant information which would affect the child's schooling.

Statementing involves getting together the opinions of the child's family and other professionals involved to decide:

> ▶ whether the child has particular needs
> ▶ whether the child will need continuous support
> ▶ what kind of support will be needed
> ▶ where that support should be offered.

The statement is a legal document and local authorities then allocate funds to support the specific needs of a child with a statement. Sometimes families don't feel that they are getting enough support and come into conflict with the local authority. When the local education authority (LEA) send a parent the final version of a statement it must also provide the name of a person who can give advice and information to the parent. It is a recommendation that a 'named person' should be discussed with parents at the early stages of the assessment process. Parents have a choice as to the individual chosen to act as their named person. Remember that the role of the named person is not the same as the named LEA Officer who acts as a source of information within the LEA.

Ideally a named person should:

▶ be a good communicator
▶ be clear if he or she disagrees with parents
▶ be contacted easily
▶ be around for several years
▶ know the parents and the child well
▶ know the education system or be willing to find out about it
▶ have some free time
▶ be good at seeing things through
▶ have no potential conflicts of interest
▶ be willing to make a long-term commitment
▶ be trusted and relied upon by parents
▶ respect confidentiality
▶ be a good listener.

The support each child is offered through his or her statement can vary from 1:1 adult contact throughout the day to perhaps an hour a day additional support for a particular subject, for example reading or maths. For the statement to be successful there needs to be the full involvement of the child's family and carers who will have strong feelings about the child's needs and will have a deep commitment to getting the best for their child.

Unfortunately the statementing process is complex and the paperwork involved is not easily accessible. You may need to explain a lot of it to parents when you are offering support to a family with a child with special educational needs. The statement should 'grow' with the individual child so that the child continues to maintain progress and develop fully. The statement includes targets that the child should achieve. These targets are set usually by the class teacher and support worker. They are usually reviewed at termly meetings where the parents are present. The targets may be complex or quite limited. For example for a child who is easily distracted a target might be that he or she should be encouraged to concentrate for longer. A child with more severe disabilities might have as a target learning how to communicate a need using a sign or gesture. Targets are very individual and at all times should be discussed with parents so that the children can be supported at home as well as at school. Review meetings are held to see whether the targets set in the statement have been reached and in order to set out new aims and future targets.

For many families this is a particularly stressful experience. Understanding and filling in forms is often a real hurdle. Many families feel the need to 'get it right' for the professionals. In fact, as professionals we need to get it right for the families! Attending meetings can also be very difficult for families. Parents can find it very painful listening to other adults talking about their own child's strengths and weaknesses. Parents often feel that the statement is mainly concerned with the things that the child **cannot** do. This makes these meetings particularly hard for parents as the tone of the conversation can seem to be quite negative.

Becoming an advocate

It can be difficult for the families to speak up for their child at this point. It may be important for you to encourage parents to take along a friend, perhaps the named person mentioned earlier. Alternatively they may want someone trained in advocacy. Perhaps you will be able to take on this role.

It is important to remember that when being an advocate for a family you are being 'the voice' for the child or parent and it needs to be at their request. It is not always possible for the child to ask for help so it may be the parent/carer who asks you on the child's behalf. Advocacy can become very important as the child gets older. There are agencies which specialise in advocacy for the parents of children with special needs and many local authorities now have services specifically set up to support the parents of these children. For example in Northamptonshire parents can find out about advocacy services through SNIX (The Special Needs Index). This is supported by the social services department under the Children Act 1989. It was set up to supply accurate information about what is available to help the family as a whole, and to help plan services for the child with special needs.

Choosing schools

At review meetings decisions are also made about the child's future schooling. This could involve mainstream school, with additional adult support, a placement in a special needs school or in a DSP – Designated Special Provision. These DSP units are often attached to a mainstream school, but have the specialised facilities of a special needs school. They may well have additional physical resources such as a hydrotherapy pool, access ramps and a higher staffing ratio within the classroom.

Choosing the right school for a child is important. Parents might need practical support if they are going to look around several schools.

Choosing a school for Michael

Three years ago as a nursery nurse, I worked with a family where there was a child, Michael, who was blind. He was leaving our nursery and his mum wanted him to go on to mainstream schooling. The process of choosing the appropriate school took up a huge amount of her time. His mum needed a great deal of support. Realistically, what could the schools offer and what long-term support was there for her son in mainstream provision? She had no transport so needed my help as I had a car. As a mum her emotions were high – not only was her son going to school, but also he was growing up and needed to go somewhere else, away from the nursery. He had spent two and a half years at nursery and she knew everyone there. She would have to tell her story again. I found it was important to actually go to visit the school with her and her son. I needed to help her to explain Michael's needs. She knew what would be best for him. I also had to pass on information from the nursery school to the primary and somehow build a bridge between the two. Michael and his mother needed to maintain the ongoing relationship and trust which had built up in nursery. Also I needed to help set up a way for Michael and his mum to finish coming to nursery so that it wasn't too painful for either of them.

Setting up a parent-friendly environment

A parent-friendly environment needs to be as welcoming as possible! Remember the wide range of needs you are catering for, and include the whole family. Be prepared to alter and change things as parents' and children's needs change over time.

> ▶ Ask parents what's useful – they know their child best. The more they can become involved the better. This may not mean staying around and being with their child all the time. They may well want and deserve a break.
> ▶ Answering difficult questions. Other children around the nursery/reception class or early years setting may often ask questions about a child with special needs who looks different. What would the child's parents like you to say in response? It's worth asking so as not to offend anyone.
> ▶ Listening to children with disabilities is very important. They know their capabilities best and will be able to make their own decisions

about whether to have a go. Limiting a child's play and development has long-term effects socially, cognitively and emotionally. You have to trust the child and give him or her the required support.

▶ Discussion. Children need to know about and understand disability and special needs. It is important not to wait until a child with a disability is part of a group before talking about it. Discussion beforehand prevents embarrassment and confusion.

▶ Have many positive images of children with special needs on display. There are different posters of both adults and children with disabilities that you can buy or are available from charities and agencies.

▶ Equipment. There are many places where you can buy specialist equipment. It is a good idea to have some of this, but remember that a lot of chairs, walkers and standing frames are made to fit individual children. Borrowing or hiring equipment is also an option. A basket of interesting materials is something that can easily be made and adapted to the needs of individual children (Goldschmied, 1987, 1994). Cardboard boxes and musical instruments are a good idea. Beanbags are ideal as they can be moulded around to physically support individual children.

▶ Buy appropriate materials. You can now buy play people with physical disabilities, with callipers and wheelchairs. This equipment should be accessible at all times, in all early years settings.

▶ Joining play schemes. These are opportunities to celebrate differences and build up the self-esteem of children with special educational needs. If possible children with special educational needs should be integrated on playschemes within their own community. Awareness can be raised, ideas exchanged and children gain hugely from spending time together. Relationships and friendships build up and sometimes children find new forms of communication with each other. This is particularly important if the majority of the child's time is spent in a special school setting. It provides an opportunity to play alongside local children. Figure 8.2 shows a letter that was written by a child who attended a community playscheme when children with special educational needs were integrated for the first time. She writes about making friends with Missy, a child who has severe speech and language difficulties and a moderate learning disability.

Thurrsday 18th Augast

Today Ive Just Arrived. Lucy and me are working with Children with Special Needs. Today I met too new friends. dawin who cant controll his temper and missy who can't say some words I felt sorry for her I would like her to be my Pen Pal I woo also would like to visit her. I Will thank lucy adventuly. It was fun with missy wer went outside up the gym we went for a walk some people were making fun of missy but it is not funny no more they can hurt their fellings. But I Like missy and dawin very much.

by Sherri Reynolds
Age 10

Figure 8.2 Making friends

Summary

▶ Children are individuals and what they **can** do needs to be celebrated first. Children with special educational needs may require additional support but have the right to a challenging and stimulating provision.
▶ Parents and children need to make the decision about what and who is most useful to them at any point in time. This means that professionals may need to stand back and listen.
▶ Parents can become the most important resource to their child with special needs. With help and support they can become passionate advocates for their children.

Bibliography

Alcott, M., (1997) An Introduction to Children with SEN. London: Hodder & Stoughton.

Andrews, E., (1996) Representing Parents at the Special Educational Needs Tribunal. Marlow: IPSEA.

Cunningham and Davis, (1985) Working with Parents: Framework for collaboration. Milton Keynes: Open University Press.

Department of Education and Science, (1978) The Warnock Report. Report of the Committee of Enquiry in the education of handicapped children and young people. London: HMSO.

DfEE, (1994) The Code of Practice on the Identification and Assessment of Special Educational Needs. London: HMSO.

Kerr, L., Sutherland, L. and Wilson, J., (1994) A Special Partnership: a practical guide for named persons and parents of children with special educational needs. Children in Scotland. HMSO: London.

Madden, P., (1995) Parents as Partners; a new perspective. British Journal of Disability, vol 23 pp 23–27.

Paterson, J., (issued annually) Disability Rights Handbook. London: Disability Alliance.

Special Educational Needs – a guide for parents. London: DfEE. In English, Bangladeshi, Chinese, Greek, Gujerati, Hindi, Punjabi, Turkish, Urdu and Vietnamese.

Wolfendale, S. (ed.), (1997) Working with Parents of SEN Children After the Code of Practice. London: David Fulton.

Useful videos

Goldschmied, E., (1987) Infants at Work. London: National Children's Bureau.

Goldschmied, E. and Hughes, A., (1994) Heuristic Play with Objects. London: National Children's Bureau.

Useful contacts

Department for Education Publications Centre, PO Box 2139, London E15.

IPSEA, PO Box 1933, Marlow, Bucks SL7 3TS.

Contact a family, 170 Tottenham Court Road, London W1P 0HA (0171 383 3555).

Parents in Partnership, 85 Trinity Avenue, Northampton NN2 6LD (01604 720062).

SNIX: Northamptonshire Special Needs Index, Northants County Council, Social Services Department, PO Box 177, County Hall, Northampton, NN1 1AY.

The Disability Alliance, First Floor East, Universal House, 88–94 Wentworth Street, London E1 7SA (0171 247 8776).

9

Daring to Care – Men and Childcare

This chapter considers the question of men's involvement in the care of young children, both as fathers and childcare workers. What are the implications for children and parents if men's involvement increases in early years settings? If it is accepted that fathers need to become more actively involved, how can early years workers achieve this when the overwhelming majority of workers are female?

The issue of gender in early years is very important. The role of men as carers, either as fathers or as early years workers, needs to be a key concern for managers and staff in any early years setting. If men are to be involved in the care of young children we have to challenge many assumptions and strongly held beliefs in our society. In this country caring for young children is still widely considered to be women's work. Despite changes in our society, the typical stereotype is that men go out to work and women look after the home and children.

Challenging stereotypes

Our society has changed significantly during the last twenty years. The traditional role of the father going out to work to provide the financial security, whilst the mother stays at home to look after the children is slowly changing. This has been partly due to developments in our industrial society where heavy industry such as mining, ship building and steel manufacturing has been replaced by lighter industries where women have more access to employment. Equal opportunity legislation has also challenged employers to open up employment opportunities to women in what were once areas of traditional male employment. Many women are now choosing to work whilst their children are under school age. In some families both parents are often working in order to maintain a standard of living that families now want and expect. This may often involve shift work or part-time work where parents will share the care of their children. More and more the relationship between parents will need to be an equal partnership with shared tasks. Shared responsibility in caring for children where both parents are actively involved in their children's upbringing can be a bonus for the whole family, although there are additional stresses involved as well.

Reconciling work and family life is essential if the well-being of the family is to be maintained. There are a number of reasons why change in the roles of parents has not been as rapid as it could have been.

Obstacles to change

Perhaps the most difficult stumbling block is the deeply held beliefs that we all have about gender – how we see ourselves as men and women and what we expect from ourselves and each other.

You could try this simple exercise to examine your own beliefs and expectations as to how men and women should behave.

EXERCISE: EXPECTATIONS OF BEHAVIOUR

1. Write down the first things that come into your head when you read the following statements.

   Boys should/shouldn't . . .   **Girls should/shouldn't . . .**

   When I think of fathers, I   **When I think of mothers, I**
   think of . . .   **think of . . .**

2. Now that you have a list of words or phrases, think about your own parents, friends and relatives and repeat the exercise using your **actual** lived experience of relationships with people that you know. You may want to do this on your own or, better still, with a small group of colleagues.

The purpose of this exercise is to separate the messages that we receive as children about how we are expected to behave as men and women, and what we actually do in practice. For example, phrases that often come up are 'boys don't cry' and 'girls shouldn't climb trees'! From these little sayings our beliefs can develop into 'men shouldn't get in touch with their feelings' and 'women mustn't do dangerous activities, they should look after others'. None of these beliefs are helpful for men or women.

These kinds of beliefs can affect the way that we respond to children, either as parents or as early years workers, on a day-to-day basis. For example how do you feel about boys dressing up in ballet dresses, shawls and bangles in their play? How do you deal with parents who come to pick their sons up and are concerned to find them wearing a dress? How much do you encourage girls to climb complex apparatus? Do girls spend equal time on the computer in your nursery?

Different countries – different systems

Our belief in the traditional roles of men and women in families is still very strong. This has been illustrated very clearly in Sweden where the government's social policy in terms of paternity leave and parental leave is very advanced compared to other European countries. Currently UK fathers have no rights to paternity leave (the male equivalent to maternity leave where the father has the right to take paid time off work when his child is born). Nor do we have parental leave where both parents are entitled to a number of days' leave to be with their children, for example to look after them when they are ill, or to attend school functions. In Sweden parents are entitled to 450 days' leave up to their child's eighth birthday and can claim 90 per cent of their salary so that they are not financially penalised for taking time off work.

Although in Sweden men are given the right to paid leave to be with their children, only 40 per cent of fathers actually take paid leave. Some of the reasons for this follow.

> ▶ Even in Sweden women are still considered to be the better carers of young children by both men and women.
> ▶ Men fear the loss of career opportunities if they take time off work, even though they are legally entitled to do so. They are afraid that their employers will not see them as committed to their work if they take leave.
> ▶ Male fear of change. Many men think that the traditional role of man as the breadwinner is at least clear. A new role requiring more active involvement and more responsibility for children leaves men feeling uncertain and therefore unsafe. For example, if caring for children is women's work, where does it leave men in terms of their masculinity if they care for children full-time?
> ▶ Female fear of change. Women felt clear about their role within the home. Their fear was that if men became more involved in childcare they would take away the role that women had traditionally held.

Should fathers be more involved?

Given these fears and worries about sharing the care of children equally, why does this issue need to be addressed in early years settings?

Benefits to parents

Society is changing, the role of the father is being challenged and some men want to be more involved in the care of their children. The children coming into the nursery may have more than one father figure. Some children will have a biological father who they see fairly regularly but will be living with their mother and her new partner. Others may be living full-time with their biological father and visiting their mother. Fathers have the same kinds of mixed feelings that mothers do about the joys and constraints of being a parent. One father expressed his joy and frustration when his child was born in this way:

> Since having Kate I've felt a lot of joy . . . a profound opening out of my soul and real connectedness with the world. I've also felt constrained and restricted, bored and angry and longed for the freedom of those days before she was born (Quoted in Seidler, 1991).

Many early years workers believe that if parents take a more equal role in bringing up children it will lead to more fulfilling family relationships. Both parents will have the same understanding of what's involved in being a parent and how becoming a parent impacts on your life on a day-to-day basis. For example, both parents need to know that it will no longer be possible to do certain things because children's needs have to come first. They will also learn new skills such as fighting for their children's rights.

It is also important for men to become more involved in childcare from an equal opportunities perspective. If men were to take an equal share in the care and upbringing of their children it would free women to take up work and develop their careers. It would also challenge employers who traditionally perceive women as risky employees (since it is women who traditionally take time off to look after their children when they are ill).

Benefits to children

If fathers took equal responsibility for childcare we might begin to see traditional stereotypes being broken down. Children are often cared for at home exclusively by women and go into settings where the staff are predominantly women. Children learn far more from what they see and experience, than from what is said to them by adults. It is not enough that fathers say they want to care for their children. They have to actually demonstrate this by taking care of them, playing with them, seeing them inside school and after school.

Parents and other important adults in children's lives, such as nursery workers, play a key role in each child's developing gender identity. If as young children they experience a world where they are cared for mainly by women, then girls will see themselves as fulfilling their role if they care for and nurture others. On the other hand, boys who grow up in a world where they are looked after almost exclusively by women may have difficulties in finding a positive male role model. Their only role model of men will be one of remote and mysterious father figures. So how do boys make sense of themselves in terms of their male identity? In their fantasy play, boys will often be seen acting out war games, being policemen or super heroes – that is, being powerful, aggressive and controlling or protecting people.

It is important for children to experience men as well as women in a variety of caring, sensitive and nurturing relationships both in the home as well as in early years education and care settings.

Political commitment

The European Union has made a longstanding commitment to a more equal sharing of family responsibilities between men and women. In March 1992, Member State Governments committed themselves to:

> promote and encourage, with due respect for freedom of the individual, increased participation by men (in the care and upbringing of children) (EC Council of Ministers Recommendation on Childcare, Article 6, 31 March 1992).

How nurseries might be more involved

Some examples from practice are given here in order to consider how early years workers could become more involved in bringing about change.

> Nursery and other services for young children can provide an important means for promoting cultural change in society, as well as providing, at a more personal level, places for safe and secure exploration of roles, relationships and identity by both men and women (Ravenna Seminar, 1993).

In 1990 Pen Green Centre for Under 5s and their Families and the Emilia-Romagna Region in Italy became jointly involved in a transnational project. The purpose of the project was to explore ways that early years settings could encourage fathers to be more involved in the care of their children.

The benefits of developing such a project in two different countries was that common strategies could be identified that were effective in different settings and cultures. At Pen Green Centre the work was based in one centre and was practitioner-led. In Emilia-Romagna Region the work was developed over the whole region and initiated by the administration.

An important starting point for the Pen Green Centre was to work with the staff group. Two basic questions were asked.

- What were we doing to enable fathers to use the centre?
- What else could we do?

Two areas were identified where immediate changes could be brought about:

- changes in the physical environment
- changes in our documentation.

The need for long-term in-service training and staff development on gender issues and practitioner research was recognised.

Physical environment

The Centre environment was very much child- and mother-focused, with photographs of women and children, children's paintings and designs and poetry by women. It was found that this did increase men's wariness about coming into the building. Several fathers had commented on the psychological and practical difficulties they had coming into the building. They were not sure how to behave, who to talk to and what to say. There was no evidence of the centre celebrating or acknowledging the role of fathers. In order to redress the balance positive images of men were provided by putting up photographic displays of fathers with their children in nursery, and a range of magazines and books were provided so that men and women felt catered for.

Documentation

Forms were rewritten specifically to include fathers rather than 'parents' (as the word 'parent' is often taken to mean 'mother'). When writing to parents both parents were named. On the application form for nursery places information on both parents' working hours was asked for so that meetings could be offered at times when **both** parents could attend. It was discovered when talking to

Marcus, a family worker in the nursery, dancing with the children

mothers that letters sent to parents would only be read by the mother. They would sometimes not inform the father about the letter because they did not think that the father would be interested. It was therefore important to arrange to talk directly with the fathers as well.

Personal and professional development

The staff spent time together in training sessions on gender issues. They wanted to raise awareness about their beliefs and values about gender. This meant that they needed to consider their own experiences of being parented and how these had influenced their views of fathers. This involved a high level of trust within the staff group and skilled trainers.

The staff at Pen Green have a long tradition of training that involves sharing personal experiences to inform and enhance their professional practice. If your staff group is not used to working in this way, then the training you offer may need to be less challenging. Early years educators need to feel confident that their concerns will be respected. They have to learn to listen to other people with different perspectives. A less intense approach might be for the staff group to watch a soap opera which involves scenes about parenting issues. In this way staff could discuss issues through a fictional portrayal of family life, avoiding the need to share personal experience. However there would still need to be some fairly personal discussion about values and beliefs.

An important learning point for staff that came out of this training was how their own upbringing continued to affect them as early years educators. Nursery staff at Pen Green found that their expectations of fathers and male workers were to some degree influenced by what they had experienced with their own fathers. Each person had been affected in different ways, even when they had similar experiences.

This is how some staff remembered their fathers:

- He was never there.
- He had more patience than my mum.
- His time was always conditional.
- He was emotionally distant.
- Dad was more emotional than mum.
- He always took on the more pleasurable aspects of looking after us, like taking us out on trips.

Impact of the training

Following their in-service training on gender, staff found that they were more open to listening to fathers. They did not make so many judgments or assumptions about how they saw fathers behaving with their children in nursery.

Because their awareness had been raised, staff were able to challenge their own assumptions. This in turn altered the way that they interacted with fathers who came into the centre. This was equally true for male staff as well as for female staff.

Practitioner research

Early years settings are all different in terms of their internal structures (how decisions are made, philosophy, ethos and levels of responsibility and the involvement that workers, parents and children have in how the provision is run), and the communities within which they work.

Practitioner research can help to sensitively change practice and make it work within the community. Individual members of staff can carry out small-scale projects linked to particular courses or interests that they are involved in.

Action research project on fathers

Angela Malcolm, a nursery nurse, decided that she would look at how work patterns and family structure influenced fathers' involvement in the care of their children. She worked with a small group of fathers in the nursery. She interviewed five fathers whose employment patterns were both 'typical' and atypical. One of the families was a traditional family with the father as the breadwinner and the mother at home with the children. In another family the roles were reversed and the mother worked full-time and the father stayed at home and cared for the children. In the third family both parents were working full-time. In the fourth family the father worked full-time and the mother worked part-time, in the evening when the father took over the care of the children. Finally she interviewed a single parent father who had chosen not to work so that he could be at home with his children.

Although this was a very small study in a very specific context, it raised some interesting issues. All the fathers felt responsible as breadwinners and felt the need to make time to be with their children. They felt the benefits for themselves when they did.

> Years ago I would not have considered it, but now that I am doing it I enjoy it very much. I now realise how much I missed out on not being around for my first three children.

All the fathers in the study expressed the need for paternity leave. They also said that they would use parental leave if it were available in the UK.

BENEFITS OF THE RESEARCH

Through interviewing fathers Angela gained a real understanding of the difficulties facing local dads. She gained an insight into the fathers' world. She saw how hard it was for them to reconcile their preoccupation with the need to earn money to provide financial security for their family, and their desire to spend time with their children. Her research had two direct benefits on the fathers involved and the nursery nurse's co-workers.

1. Fathers felt equally valued as parents and felt that the staff saw their role as fathers as very important. The nursery nurse represented the family centre and gave an important message to the family that the centre was committed to listening to fathers as well as mothers and that staff wanted fathers to be involved and supported by the centre as much as possible.
2. Her research helped the whole staff group to develop a deep understanding of family life and the importance of the father's role, helping them to value fathers and have a clearer understanding of how fathers were thinking and experiencing their role as parents. Practical changes to the nursery's routines were made to encourage fathers to be more involved, for example running meetings so that fathers on shifts could attend in the evening and making sure that male staff helped to run meetings.

Improving practice by using video tapes

Video recording can provide useful information on how adults actually interact with each other, rather than how they think they do! In order to

Aisha says goodbye to her dad Abdul, as she plays outside on her favourite toy.

gather information about how staff greeted parents when they brought their children to a nursery, the staff set up a video camera to record parents coming in. The beginning of each session is a crucially important time for parents if they are to feel welcome and comfortable leaving their child in the care of others.

When the video tapes were analysed staff found that there was a lot more eye contact between the staff and the mothers. Staff also stood closer to mothers and sometimes made physical contact with them. With fathers there was more physical distance and much less time was spent talking to staff. Nursery staff tended to talk and chat longer and in more depth with mothers than with fathers. The quality of contact between staff and fathers was not as rich. Watching the video tapes and discussing what staff saw themselves doing raised their awareness. It helped workers to take some responsibility for the poorer quality of their interactions with fathers and do something about it. Now nursery staff make more eye contact, initiate more conversations with fathers and offer fathers more support. Fathers are tending to stay longer in nursery and have said that they feel more comfortable bringing their children in now that they know the staff better.

Clearly the process of making fathers feel more welcome doesn't happen overnight. It has to proceed at the fathers' own pace and in a way that leaves nursery staff feeling comfortable.

Male workers in childcare provision

In Scandinavian countries researchers have found that employing more male workers has:

> ▶ improved the quality of childcare services
> ▶ enabled the curriculum to become more varied. For example, in childcare centres where there were equal numbers of men and women employed, researchers found that all children occupy themselves more with activities involving construction and movement
> ▶ increased the activity of both boys and girls in social games and increased the amount of dialogue between children and adults, and adults and adults
> ▶ caused staff groups to function better and make decisions more quickly. Gender differences between men and women were valued
> ▶ caused increased participation by the children's fathers.

The impact on children

As significant adults in the lives of children early years workers need to be aware of the messages that they can give to children about their gender identity. Some of these messages are more obvious than others. In David Panter's study (1992) of adult/child interactions he observed that when a child was involved in gender-related play, the adult would reinforce their behaviour by saying, 'good boy', or 'good girl'. If their play was not gender-specific the adult would say, 'well done' without using the words 'girl' or 'boy'.

The difficulty of identifying such behaviour is that staff are often not aware that they are doing it. For example, in a nursery the staff were looking for photographs of girls to illustrate their autonomy and self-confidence. The photographs that had been collected of children on the climbing frame showed all the boys climbing on their own. All the girls had a member of staff holding their hand!

Close observation of adult/child interactions are vital if staff are to raise their awareness of how to reinforce or challenge gender stereotypes in the children they care for.

Encouraging men to work in the early years

There are clear advantages to increasing the number of male workers in early year settings. Research has shown that the vast majority of workers welcome more male childcare workers. The NCH Action for Children commissioned research into 77 family centres and found that 86 per cent of staff were in favour of more male workers. In her review of research into the impact of male workers in early years settings, Jensen (1993) concluded that where there were few male workers, staff would discuss why and if men should be employed. Where there were already a significant number of male workers the discussion would centre around how to increase the number of men employed in early years work.

Studies have shown that children are more likely to be influenced by the gender of their adult carers when they are in nursery. This influence is significantly less when the child goes to school. By the age of five, children are more fixed in their thinking about how they should behave as boys or girls so this makes it even more important that men should be involved in early years settings.

There is some evidence, however, that for men to have an impact in early years settings there should be at least 20 per cent male workers in the staff group. This would prevent male workers feeling isolated and give them some of the support they need.

> **Whether or not the male worker is consciously troubled by male stereotypes, he must navigate in a world full of them; at almost every step he must contradict them. In doing so he somehow must not feel like an occupational failure, or like a pet rabbit – the exceptional male at the childcare centre (Seifert, 1974).**

Concerns and fears

The main concern that staff express about involving men in childcare is the possibility of child abuse – in particular, child sexual abuse. This is an

Sticky tape is useful if you want to envelop your family worker – and keep him where you want him!

extremely emotive issue. The majority of men involved in early years work are caring and committed workers. However there have been cases where men have abused children, which does raise the important question of should men be employed in childcare no matter how small the risk? The consequences of abuse are devastating for the child, his or her family and the workers. Children have a right to be in a safe and secure environment and if parents are entrusting the care of their children to day carers, then staff must ensure that they receive high quality education and care. There are some important issues to be considered.

> ▶ **The power of abuse lies in secrecy.** If the culture of the early years centre is based on empowerment and openness then the potential for abuse will be minimised.
>
> ▶ **There should be careful staff selection procedures.** Police checks are not enough as only an estimated 2 per cent of offenders are ever convicted of offences. The organisation Children in Scotland has made a number of recommendations detailing who should interview candidates and how they should be interviewed.

> ▶ **There should be parental involvement in the services that are provided.** Parents, both mothers and fathers, care about the quality of care that their children will have. There needs to be the opportunity for parents to meet with staff to share information and raise questions about how the service can be improved. If the early years setting has a structure that encourages open communication between workers and families and people feel actively listened to and valued, then it is more likely that any form of abuse would be quickly identified and appropriately handled.

Some parents may feel wary and confused by a male worker caring for their child. We hear stories in the media about the abuse of children, mainly by men, and this may cause apprehension on the part of parents. How do parents know if their fears are unwarranted? How would you feel if your child was starting nursery and you found that their carer was a man? Early years workers need to effectively reassure the parents and help them to feel comfortable. Empowerment is about involving parents in the shared care of their children. If parents feel listened to and have a real say in how their child is cared for, then they will feel reassured. It is important that their fears are acknowledged and respected.

STAFF TRAINING

In order to protect children, staff training is vital and should include sessions on:

> ▶ how children communicate: children are very sensual and naturally relate to adults and each other using all their senses
> ▶ child development, including early sexual development
> ▶ how physical, sexual and emotional abuse occurs and how to recognise signs of abuse in children
> ▶ personal and professional development which enables staff to take responsibility and deal with their own issues.

ASSERTIVENESS PROGRAMMES FOR CHILDREN, STAFF AND PARENTS

Assertiveness courses are very popular with parents who want to develop their skills and self-confidence. This is also true for staff in early years settings. Childcare is undervalued in our society and childcare workers often feel taken for granted. They need to find their voice.

Children can also benefit from assertiveness programmes designed for three and four year olds to encourage autonomy and develop self-confidence.

Working with fathers

The way in which you work with fathers and the services that you offer depends upon the context within which you work and the needs of the local community.

TRAINING

An important starting point is with staff themselves. Training is needed to develop expertise, understanding, and self-confidence. To encourage men to be more involved in the care of children is to bring about a fundamental change in our society. Belief systems and values need to be explored and challenged by the whole staff group. Remember that this is an ongoing area of training which needs to be repeated each year or whenever there are new members of staff joining the team.

PARENT FORUMS

Meetings between staff and parents (where men and women can share ideas) need to be arranged in order to share ideas and feelings about fathers' involvement and the implications of having male workers in early childcare settings.

These are the sort of concerns that have been raised in discussions.

> ▶ The setting can be seen by some women as a safe haven, where they can get support for themselves. Many women have experienced difficult and damaging relationships with men and expressed their concern about men using the centre and what the implications might be – for example, if men begin to take over and dominate groups. In practice this has not happened and most parents and staff have reported that having more men around has been helpful in challenging stereotypical assumptions.
> ▶ Parents have specifically asked that the nursery has more male workers as they feel their children will miss out on experiencing positive, caring relationships with men. When advertising for new posts some nurseries now include this statement, 'we would welcome applications from men'.

GROUPWORK

Men's groups can be effective ways of introducing fathers into nurseries. These groups can give men an opportunity to:

> ▶ overcome their feelings of isolation. Groups offer members a safe forum within which to share personal feelings and their hopes and fears as parents and individuals
> ▶ raise gender awareness and to take personal responsibility for how they relate to each other, to women and to children
> ▶ explore issues around being a man and what male identity means
> ▶ provide a safe forum within which to develop trusting relationships.

Groups can also address many important issues including dealing with stress, relationships, self-esteem, health, aggression, alcohol and drug abuse. One group member responded in this way when he was asked 'what have you gained from attending the group?'

> A better life, a sense of well-being. A source of support and motivation in keeping with my own set of beliefs and values. It is without doubt the only place in which I can explore my strengths and weaknesses without being judged . . .

THE FATHERS' GROUP

Fathers may want a group specifically to look at issues about being a father. In one nursery group members were varied: one was a grandfather who had taken on the primary care of his grandchildren, another was a single parent father, and another was a stepfather as well as a natural father. Issues that have arisen in this group include the difficulties men face when they take on the primary care of their children. The welfare and legal system still works on the assumption that women are the primary carers of their children and all the men in this group had experienced discriminatory practice. They had also experienced negative remarks in their day-to-day contact with people, such as 'you should get a proper job and not waste your time bringing your children to school'.

Summary

> ▶ Working with fathers and addressing issues of gender in our work with children is very important. Although some of the issues are complicated in this chapter ideas are provided that can easily be put into practice and can be effective.

▶ Early years workers can play an important part in involving and valuing fathers and breaking down stereotypes. The inequalities that exist are not good for men, women or children. Children need to be able to express themselves without being inhibited by gender stereotyping. If a boy is upset it is important that no-one tells him 'big boys don't cry'. Girls need to grow up believing that they have the right to express their angry feelings. Children have a strong sense of justice and are naturally in touch with how they feel. They need to be encouraged and supported in expressing and trusting their feelings.

▶ Although there are concerns about men which need to be addressed, the majority of fathers and male workers are committed to caring for and protecting their children.

▶ Children need to experience caring, sensitive men in early years settings. Boys need positive role models and girls need to develop healthy expectations about how men can be.

▶ Mothers are still generally regarded as the natural carers of their children. If a father works long hours or is separated from his partner, he may have little contact with his children. Unless there are issues of abuse or violence it is important for children to spend time with their fathers. Having a positive male role model at home helps boys to develop self-confidence and feel positive about their masculinity and who they are.

▶ There is growing evidence in the UK and in other European countries that parents, children and workers want to see more men involved in childcare. Early years workers can play an important part in this process by making early years settings more men friendly. We need to make our settings more accessible to those fathers and male workers who want to be involved.

▶ We must take into account the cultural and religious backgrounds of the families we are working with. This may be particularly important with minority ethnic groups as in some cultures the roles of men and women are highly differentiated. A male worker was talking with a mother of a child in the nursery who is a Muslim. They were sitting in a study room and discussing her GCSE Psychology coursework when she said, 'If only my friends could see me talking with you on our own and as equals because they would not believe this was possible – and I wouldn't have believed it a year ago either!'

Bibliography

Cacace, M. and d'Andrea, L., (1996) Fathers in Services for Young Children. Good practices in sharing responsibility between men and women. Rome: European Childcare Network.

Jalmert, L., (1990) Increasing Men's Involvement as Fathers in the Care of their Children – Some Gains and Obstacles in Men as Carers for Children. Report of a seminar held in Glasgow, May 1990. European Childcare Network (ed).

Jensen, J.J., (1993) Men as Carers. Discussion paper presented at Ravenna, Italy May 21–22. European Childcare Network.

Malcolm, A., (1992) Father's Involvement with their Children and Outside Commitments. Unpublished paper for Advanced Diploma in Child Care and Education.

Panter, D., (1992) 'Men as Carers'. Conference at Pen Green Centre, 1992. Unpublished paper.

Ravenna Seminar, (1993) Men as Carers – Towards a culture of responsibility, sharing and reciprocating between women and men in the care and upbringing of children. European Childcare Network.

Ruxton, S., (1992) What's he doing at the Family Centre? The Dilemmas of Men who Care for Children. National Children's Homes.

Seidler, V.J., (1991) The Achilles Heel Reader: Men, Sexual Politics and Socialism. London: Routledge.

Seifert, K. (1974) 'Some Problems of Men in Child Care Centre Work' in Men and Masculinity (eds Pleek, J. and Sawyer, J.) Englewood Cliffs: Prentice Hall.

Fathers, Nurseries and Childcare. European Commission Network on Children. Network Coordinator: Peter Moss, Thomas Coram Research Unit, 27/28 Woburn Square, London WC1H 0AA.

10

Parents as Life-long Learners

Since I've had kids I've been stuck in the house like a gerbil . . . rushing up and down cleaning till I was blue in the face . . . I need something to look forward to . . .

If you are working with young children you are also working with their parents. The scale of involvement you have will depend on your work setting and your personal approach. This chapter shows ways of working more closely with parents as learners. It also gives concrete examples of parents' experiences as learners within a number of different early childhood settings.

Defining learning

For the purpose of this chapter, learning is everything a person comes to know, understand, assimilate and value. Learning always belongs to the learner. It is both knowledge we go to find out – for example, how to plan an activity for children – as well as knowledge which is about a discovery – for example, that you can speak out in a group of people and say what you really believe.

Being careful not to label

Who are we talking about when we say 'parents'? There is always a problem of labelling and thereby stereotyping people. Who do you think of when you say 'parent': do you think about men or do you think about women? One of the comments often made by parents returning to education is, 'I want to find me again.' When we talk about parents in this chapter we mean any adults involved in the care of children – whether parents, step-parents, parents' partners, foster parents – who want to have a second chance in education.

Identifying parent's needs

Thinking of parents as life-long learners is important in the early years setting for a number of reasons.

▶ As children enter school parents begin to question their lifestyles and think, 'what about me?' and 'I want something for me ...'.

▶ This is often a time when parents reflect on their own educational experience and their own educational and learning needs.

▶ Parents often feel the need to develop themselves in order to support their children's learning.

▶ It is a time when parents, particularly women, feel most lost, vulnerable and isolated. In early childhood settings we need to have a flexible and responsive approach to working with parents. We need to offer support to parents whose self-esteem is often at rock bottom.

▶ Key workers in early childhood settings are in a unique position to enable parents to get involved in learning as adults.

Parents who try to return to traditional and rigid educational settings when their children start school are often disappointed. Old methods of teaching and learning involving set timetables, exams and very strict deadlines are removed from the rest of the parent's life. The hopeful parent returning to learning often feels lost. His or her feelings of failure are reinforced. Early childhood settings can have a very positive impact in helping parents in their learning process. New integrated centres for children and families are currently being set up, in the tradition of Margaret McMillan (see chapter 1), often funded by the local authority with additional finance from the European Community central government funding such as the Single Regeneration Fund. In these early years centres parents will be encouraged to learn while their children are receiving part-time or full-time education and care. In some of these centres there will also be a strong focus on adults wanting to return to training or employment. They could be offered training courses within these settings and the chance to embark on training for jobs in childcare. An integrated approach offers parents a chance they may not have had before. Their learning can happen within a supportive setting which acknowledges them and their individual needs. In this way adult community education can take place alongside early childhood education and care. In traditional nursery schools and classes, day nurseries or playgroups it is also possible to work in this way. Workers in these settings are in a key position to enable parents to take a first step on a career route.

Parents speaking out

The following stories are told by parents who are reflecting on their learning and educational experience within early years settings. The opportunities they were offered helped them to go on and become paid workers in childcare settings.

Marcus wanted to train as a childcare worker and got involved through a local authority nursery school which was also an NVQ assessment centre.

In the third year at school when you had to pick options, I picked the 14–16 option, which meant I left school with no English or maths. I was not put forward for exams. I stayed on for another year and did a certificate in pre-vocational caring, which covered aspects of care. I made my decision from that, that I wanted to work with children – and applied for the NNEB. I think the 14–16 option let me down. I never really understood it. I realised I wanted to work with children but felt that school had failed me.

I did my NNEB for two years at college and failed my exams. I had just had enough by then and wasn't wanting to do childcare then or resit. I went to work in a factory for $2\frac{1}{2}$ years doing warehouse packing. It was physically hard work – packing cases of lager and wine. Then I got made redundant when the company closed down.

One day I was at the nursery where I had done my NNEB placement. I was meeting my partner who worked in the playgroup there. One of the nursery staff asked me if I would like to do supply work for them. So I began working there sessionally. I was given the opportunity to do the NVQ in Childcare and Education based at the nursery. The head of the nursery approached me and explained it all to me. What swayed me was that I could do it while I was actually doing my job and wouldn't have to do loads of writing unless I wanted to. I felt college was much more isolated – here, I was working alongside these people and I could ask them things as I needed to and we were working together. Not having to do an exam relieved an enormous feeling of pressure.

I went on to achieve my NVQ Level 3 and am now working full-time as a nursery worker. I also went on to do English GCSE and passed it, and am still working on my maths. I feel better about myself – as a father to two children, I wanted to be able to support them. Now I've started doing an early years degree course which is through distance learning. Five or six of us are doing it together.

Suzy is a young parent who found that the help and support she received from her health visitor and staff in a local centre for under fives and families enabled her to find what she was good at doing and could achieve.

My name is Susan, but I prefer to be called Suzy. I am 27 years old and have lived in Corby all my life. I was educated up to O level standard in English and up to CSE standard in other subjects such as maths and RE. School was crap! The teachers were more interested in what side of the corridor you walked down than what you were achieving in the classroom.

I left school and met John and began work in Kentucky Fried Chicken, and then in a cosmetic packaging factory. I became pregnant and was signed off work as I was having a difficult pregnancy with Natasha. John and I split up when she was three months old.

I stayed with my Mum until Natasha was five months old and we were allocated a house. My health visitor wanted me to start mixing with other mothers as I was only eighteen and on my own in a new area of town. She took me to the local Centre for Under Fives and families to look around and I joined a group run by parents for parents and their children. I immediately loved the Centre and I attended the group every week. In the meantime I had reconciled with John and a year later was pregnant. Again I was really ill and told to have complete rest.

Damian was born four days after Natasha's second birthday. The staff at the hospital were happy with him, although I was not. We were discharged when he was 48 hours old. Less than 24 hours later I was back in hospital, this time in Special Care. From there to the John Radcliffe in Oxford where Damian died aged four days old of a heart condition. I was devastated and incapable of doing anything. Time passed and again my health visitor came to my rescue. She enrolled me on an Open University course – the Pre-School Child Course at the nursery centre. I met the supervisor of the playgroup and got on really well with her – she suggested that working in the playgroup may help take my mind off Damian. Natasha came to playgroup with me and I worked there for four mornings a week. I felt like a natural. It finally felt like I belonged somewhere. When it was time for Natasha to go into the main nursery I began to do crèche work. John and I had split up again. Natasha was almost ready to start school when I decided that children played a major part in my life – they are so wonderful to watch and work with and I get great pleasure from seeing them grow and learn. I made enquiries about Employment Training and found I could get a qualification by having a placement in the nursery centre and doing a course at the local college. I worked as a crèche co-ordinator for six months, working towards my goal. During this time I met my partner, Andy, and was really starting to look forward to the future. Unfortunately Employment Training failed me by not providing the promised books and generally not being able to deliver what they said they could. Funding was only for one year and with delays in providing books, and so on, I had to leave the course. I was extremely disheartened, considering the amount of time and energy I had put in. I even left the Centre and spent most of my time in the house.

In 1991 I had another baby, Sara. Once again most of my pregnancy was spent in and out of hospital. I started using the baby massage group at the Centre and the Writer's Group (my other passion). Being back in the Centre brought back how close my qualification had been and I began to think about trying again. In 1992 I found that I was expecting again. This time my health wasn't too bad, but it was scary when the scans revealed that I was having a baby boy – all the memories of Damian came flooding back. I gave birth to Martin and now that he is a bit older I feel this is the right time to do something for me.

Having a childcare qualification has always been my ambition and always seemed to be out of reach until now. I've now got my NVQ in Childcare and Education Level 2 and I'm working towards my NVQ Level 3 at the Centre. It feels like there is nothing to stand in my way and my determination is even stronger now.

Parents access learning in different ways

Marcus and Suzy both benefited from being able to use the kinds of early years services where staff listened and tried to respond to parents' expressed needs. They both made their own decisions about what they wanted to do and did it in their own time. For both of them there were weeks where they

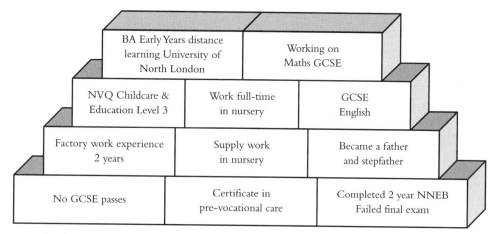

BA Early Years distance learning University of North London	Working on Maths GCSE	
NVQ Childcare & Education Level 3	Work full-time in nursery	GCSE English
Factory work experience 2 years	Supply work in nursery	Became a father and stepfather
No GCSE passes	Certificate in pre-vocational care	Completed 2 year NNEB Failed final exam

Figure 10.1 Marcus' route through early years training

felt they had taken two steps back for each step forward but they both had clear goals. Their schooling had left them with low self-esteem and few, if any, qualifications. Now as adult learners they were ready to take responsibility for their own learning.

It may be useful to look back to chapter 1 where parents' different routes through early years services were discussed.

Whilst Marcus' route (see figure 10.1) was fairly clear in that he wanted to secure a childcare qualification the nursery was useful in that it offered him more support than he had found in a traditional FE College setting. Suzy's route (figure 10.2) was more circuitous. She needed a lot of practical support and confidence building. She has gone on to run groups for other parents and at the same time establish some stepping stones for her own career in education and care. Both parents used their adult learning experiences to:

▶ share anxieties
▶ build up their own self-esteem
▶ make supportive friendships.

What drives us and what holds us back?

It is very important for you as an early childhood educator to understand what holds parents back when they seem on the brink of taking a step forward into adult learning. It is also important to acknowledge what drives

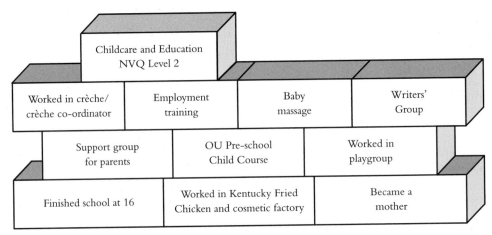

Figure 10.2 Suzy's route through early years training

them on. Think about Suzy's situation. What drives her as an adult learner? What holds her back? Figure 10.3 summarises another nursery parent's experience of trying to access adult education.

Perhaps you can remember how you felt on leaving school. What drove you on to follow your career path; what held you back? If you understand your own motivation and can get in tune with what blocked you or helped you then you'll be better able to understand the parents in your setting.

Whatever your setting we hope you will feel inspired after reading about Marcus and Suzy to begin to set up some kind of adult learning experience for parents. In urban areas where nurseries have been able to secure external funding they have set up small scale projects which can support up to twenty adult learners at a time. You may not want to work with such large numbers to start with but it is useful to have a vision of what you may be able to achieve in the future. You might want to start by getting parents to tell you how they felt about their own schooling – perhaps you could design a questionnaire to use at a parents' evening.

Setting up a programme to help parents back into employment

The Wider Opportunities for Learning Project

One nursery centre set up a project to give parents the space and time to look at their own learning needs. The idea for the project came from listening to what parents were saying and from working alongside parents in

Driving circumstances permitting What drives you on as an adult learner? +	Restraining circumstances constraining What holds you back? -
Anxiety and desire to be a 'good enough' parent Doesn't want a boring job Wants to be able to say 'this woman lived, not just existed' Wants something to believe in Wants to take something for herself Able to believe in myself Wants to use her experience of having things taken away from her Wants to show people she can achieve Has supportive friends and supportive professionals	Loneliness and desperation Practical problems: cost, babysitting, distance Previous bad/painful experiences of education/teachers Personal lack of confidence, low self-esteem

Figure 10.3 Permitting and restraining circumstances

the nursery. Staff with the help of their local social services department applied for and received funding through the European Social Fund. The funding was specifically focused on helping unemployed parents get back into employment. Such funding is given on the condition that centres adhere to very strict guidelines.

Nursery parents said they realised that while they were giving a lot of their time and energy and enjoying helping out in nursery, they were unqualified and therefore unable to secure paid employment in the childcare field.

Other parents expressed the view that they felt in limbo, they had young children and wanted to do something for themselves, but didn't know what. They were scared to make the wrong decision and so couldn't do anything. When parents were asked to talk about how they felt about their schooling most parents expressed feelings of low self-esteem and a lack of confidence.

Over 50 per cent had left school at 16 and felt that the school system had let them down.

The Wider Opportunities Project's aim was to respond to what parents said they needed. It was important for the project to help build parental self-esteem and confidence and to acknowledge the vast range of experience and skills parents brought with them when their children started nursery.

It was also important that the project offered parents a realistic way back into education and employment with small steps that they felt they could achieve. One of the parents described her previous experience of trying to return to college as an adult learner:

I looked in the local paper where courses were advertised and picked psychology because it interested me. I went along to sign up and waited in different queues – I really wanted to ask someone about it first, but anyway I just filled in the forms. The first night I was terrified – I didn't know anyone. I went a couple of times, but the effort to get there – getting someone to babysit – made it impossible. I just felt guilty and silly.

Adult learners working together

It was important that this new project should offer parents a more positive experience of returning to education, training and work. Initially the project offered parents the opportunity to come and talk with a project worker about themselves and their interests. Because the project had external funding the parents who got involved were given practical help such as crèche facilities, travel expenses, course fees and any educational materials that they required.

After initial vocational guidance and counselling was offered to parents, most began moving in their chosen directions. Parents said what they needed and project workers tried to respond to these needs. Usually what parents wanted was a mixture of vocational and personal development training. The project grew and developed with the parents who took part in it. See figure 10.4 for an example outline of a session plan.

Remember:
- This is a first tentative step for most parents.
- Parents may be very nervous.
- It took a lot for them to even come at all.

1. Arrival
   Quick discussion to put parents at ease.
   How did you arrive?
   How are you feeling?
   What have you done already today?

2. Getting to know each other
   Share common interests.

3. Giving information
   Discussion about NVQ in Childcare and Education
   How does it work?

4. Future wider opportunities sessions
   What will be available?
   What might people want?

5. Quick round up

Figure 10.4 Outline of a session plan

Parents who took part in the project commented on aspects that worked for them.

'I've gained invaluable experience, confidence and support in finding my direction from being on the course.' (Helena Georgiou)

'I am able to work at my own pace, with no pressure like there has been with other courses. I feel I'm working harder on this than I have on any other course. The flexibility means I can still put the kids first and do my own work.' (Suzy Bennett)

'My self-confidence has increased greatly since I joined the project. The insight into children's behaviour is so enjoyable. I wish I had done this course when my own children were young.' (Maria Farren)

'Knowing that Kalya was happy in the crèche helped me to relax into the course. The tutors were more relaxed, more like friends than teachers. I could express myself without feeling judged.' (Lynn Wilson)

Rhama learned about the Project when she visited the nursery.

Rhama joined the Project and spent a number of weeks meeting and talking about herself and the areas of work she was interested in. She had experience as a volunteer worker escorting adults with special needs but didn't really want to work in that field. She expressed feelings of failure regarding her past educational experience, was worried about being accepted in professional environments and was scared to hope.

She was interested in working with young children and began a placement in a community-run playgroup. She joined the NVQ in Childcare and Education Programme and began to work towards a Level 2 award.

Rhama expanded her work placement experience during the course time – working sessionally in a playgroup; working as a classroom assistant in an infant school and setting up and running a group for parents and children that ran once a week. She also requested training and help in putting together her CV and gaining interview skills which helped to boost her confidence.

Rhama's confidence grew stronger over the period of time she was on the project. She achieved her NVQ

Level 2 qualification and is currently working towards her NVQ Level 3 independently of the project. In her own words:

> The Wider Opportunities Project gave me confidence after being at home for a long time. I could be myself, I wasn't just somebody's mother. I was doing what I enjoyed. If it wasn't for going there I don't know what I'd be doing.

The NVQ in Childcare and Education Award

Many parents who got involved in the project were interested in actually gaining a qualification in childcare. The project offered them the opportunity to gain an NVQ in Childcare and Education Levels 2 and 3 as the nursery was also an assessment centre. Parents attended group sessions which covered the core units of the NVQ and staff offered parents help in gathering and collating work for their portfolios. Project workers also encouraged a discussion-based approach where parents were actively involved and able to share their own experiences and skills.

Adult learning – a balancing act

> 'Significant learning combines the logical and the feelings,
> the concept and the experience,
> the idea and the meaning.' (Rogers, 1983)

This quotation by Carl Rogers highlights to some extent the philosophy of the project's work in enabling parents' return to learning. The Wider Opportunities Project is an example of the kind of lifelong learning where parents found that their 'feelings', their 'experience' and their 'meaning' mattered.

The Wider Opportunities Project grew and developed ways of working with parents during four years and was very successful. Parents could attend group sessions about their own needs as parents and learners and then attend courses which supported them in taking up NVQs in Childcare and Education. The content of the course built on and developed skills and experience that parents had already gained, such as noticing and observing their children's play. Then they had opportunities to undertake placements and be assessed for their NVQ in the same nursery centre alongside other qualified childcare workers.

Even if your setting is not in a position to directly offer NVQs perhaps you could run a short course on building parents' self-esteem or on helping parents to find a focus as adult learners. Then you could identify a local college or an NVQ assessment centre where parents could go on working towards accreditation.

Your role in an education and care setting

At the beginning of this chapter it was stated that if you are working with children you will be working with their parents. When a childcare worker listens and enables a parent to develop his or her learning needs it will inevitably have a positive impact on the children in their care. Everything is connected – everything links. Involving parents, working alongside parents and sharing the care of children with parents is a core part of the work of any early childhood educator. In this chapter we have tried to recognise the many roles that parents take on. The Wider Opportunities Project particularly focuses on womens' role as 'other than mother' (MacLachlan, 1996). Other chapters in this book have described in detail how parents, both fathers and mothers, can be involved in daily routines within our early childhood settings. Engaging parents as active partners does however mean that we must recognise the pressures parents face whether unemployed, working full-time or working part-time. We must recognise the fact that parents can show their commitment to their children in many different ways, not just in the home or in helping out in nursery or by attending groups. Helping parents to see themselves as lifelong learners is also important and there are practical things that early childhood educators can do to help parents on their journey.

This chapter ends with a poem written by a woman who reflects on her learning experiences.

I WATCHED THE CAT UNCURL

We all finished Senior School
They became everything I was not
Strong, confident and coping with their lot
They followed education's path, GCSEs, degrees to the top
I married, had children, was statistically forgot
They came back fresh, hungry and ready for the world
I changed nappies, burped babies and watched the cat uncurl

They bought houses, got married on settled ground
I picked up my pencil and pad, finally became educationally sound
They didn't cheer or egg me on, but who needs them when I feel strong

Maxine McKay

Summary

> ▶ Know or have access to information regarding local educational establishments – both non-traditional and traditional.
>
> ▶ Know or have information regarding how to apply for funding to set up parent projects, for example contact your local social services or education department about the possibility of tapping into European funding. Contact your local adult basic education department or the Workers Educational Association (WEA).
>
> ▶ Identify your own professional development needs regarding working with parents – for example, developing listening skills.
>
> ▶ Be your own researcher. For example, visit other childcare settings and find out how other settings are offering learning and education opportunities to parents.
>
> ▶ Observe what happens in your own setting and begin thinking about ways to improve things so that you can be more responsive to the learning needs of parents.

Bibliography

Fletcher, C., (1987) Community Education: An Agenda for Educational Reform (ed, Allen, G.). Milton Keynes: Open University Press.

Flynn, P. (et al) (1986) (ed) You're Learning All the Time: Women, Education and Community Work. Nottingham: Spokesman.

MacLachlan, K., (1996) Good Mothers are Women too in Bastiani, J., and Wolfendale, S., (eds) Home School Work in Britain. London: David Fulton.

Northedge, A., (1990) The Good Study Guide. Milton Keynes: Open University Press.

Rogers, C., (1983) Freedom to Learn for the 80s. Merrill: McMillan USA.

Walkerdine, V. and Lucey, H., (1989) Democracy in the kitchen. London: Virago.

Whalley, M., (1994) Learning to be Strong – Integrating Education and Care in Early Childhood. London: Hodder & Stoughton.

Useful contacts

European Social Fund & Single Regeneration Fund – contact local LEA or local authority social services department.

The Basic Skills Agency, 7th Floor Commonwealth House, 1–19 New Oxford Street, London WC1A 1NU (0171 405 4017).

Workers Educational Association, (Eastern District), Botolph House, 17 Botolph Lane, Cambridge CB2 3RE (0223 350978).

Donna Vizma, Wider Opportunities Project, Pen Green Centre for Under 5's & Families, Pen Green Lane, Corby, Northants NN17 1BJ (01536 400068).

Council for Awards in Children's Care & Education (CACHE), 8 Chequer Street, St Albans, Herts AL1 3XZ (01727 847636).

Conclusion

The UK needs a new strategy that simultaneously meets the needs of young children and extends their parents' choices; under fives provision is good for children, good for parents and good for the economy and society (The Report for Commission on Social Justice, 1994).

What are the key messages for early childhood educators who want to actively involve parents in what is going on in their settings?

> ▶ **You need to recognise the great untapped energy and ability of all parents using our settings. You need to have high expectations of their interest in and commitment to their children's learning.**
> ▶ **You need to develop mutual understanding and share experiences with parents.**
> You can do this through:
>
> - home visiting
> - providing parent-friendly spaces within your setting
> - offering parents a range of groups that focus on their own learning needs and their children's learning needs
> - encouraging parents to run services for others and take on management roles in your setting.
>
> ▶ **You have to clearly articulate your values and beliefs and your methods of working.**
>
> If you aren't clear about what you are doing and why you are doing it then it will be hard for you to have the confidence to let parents in.
>
> ▶ **You need to recruit staff to work in early years settings who are confident, articulate, well trained and as excited about working with parents as they are about working with children.**
>
> To work effectively with parents you need a range of skills that you may not have been taught on your initial training courses.

Working with parents you need to be able to:

- negotiate
- listen
- manage conflicts and crisis
- be an effective advocate
- try to be non-judgmental
- act as a referee
- empathise
- make quick decisions
- reflect
- set good clear boundaries.

A good starting-off point in your setting would be to set time aside for a training session. Identify which members of staff have skills, strengths and experience in working with parents, and who needs additional training. Then you'll need to develop a comprehensive training strategy for working with parents.

▶ **If you want to establish an equal, active and responsive partnership with parents then the work with parents has to be driven by those parents who already use the services and those parents who say they would like to use them.**

Parents may want to spend time writing about their children in the style of a 'baby biography'. Alternatively, they may just want to attend a once-a-week session to find out more about their children's educational needs. They may want to use your early years setting for support for themselves as parents, or as a place to come and play with a young sibling. They may want to run services themselves or be on a management group or governing body within the setting. They may well be working full-time and only be able to attend meetings infrequently or in the evening. Or they may want to spend many hours each day in the early years setting. **You must always be aware that to put parents under pressure to attend and get involved is to be coercive: 'the iron fist in a velvet glove'. On the other hand, if you don't make your services welcoming, open and responsive they may continue to feel that there is no place for them in their child's early years setting. The parents' level of involvement must always be their decision, and the timing and pace of their involvement is in their hands.**

▶ **That working with parents in the ways described in this book is always political.**

Chapter 1 referred to Margaret McMillan, an educator who worked at the beginning of this century. She believed that it was possible to create a more just society through early years education and education for parents. Professor Chris Pascal was also quoted as a modern-day advocate for children and parents who said that we should encourage parents 'to stop accepting their lot and start creating the world they would like to be part of'. The late Paulo Freire, a powerful community educator, described this process very clearly as being about opening up for parents a 'language of possibilities'. All early childhood educators work in a different context with different constraints. However, we can all be part of this kind of process. With a change in government and a new millennium perhaps it will be possible for there to be a new approach to working with children and families where we can meet the needs of children, offer support to their parents and also extend parents' choices.

Bibliography

Freire, P., (1974) Pedagogy of the Oppressed. London: Penguin.

Rogers, C., (1983) Freedom to learn for the '80s. Merrill: McMillan USA.

Social Justice Strategies for National Renewal, (1994) The Report of the Commission on Social Justice. London: Vintage.

Glossary

Advocate – someone who is prepared to speak up on behalf of a child

Agenda – items the participants discuss at a meeting

Awarding Body – award qualifications in child care and education, e.g. CACHE and BTEC

Candidate – any student, male or female, full-time or part-time, mature or young

Cognitive concerns – matters to do with knowledge

Conservation of number – the principle that the total quantity of objects remains the same if none are added or taken away

Curriculum – what is offered to young children in nursery and how and why certain provision is offered

Deep level learning – what is taking place inside a learner when learning results in a shift in understanding or outlook. Children are always very involved when deep level learning takes place

Early years worker or educator – anyone qualified by training or experience to work in childcare or education

Enclosure – a rotational movement resulting in a closed shape

Exploration – the search for new knowledge and understanding

Heuristic play – developed from the work of Elinor Goldschmied, this involves children from 12 months to 2 years in playing very deliberately with a limited range of objects which they can sort, fit and touch

Involvement – when deeply involved, a person shows concentration, persistence and high levels of self-motivation

Intrinsic motivation – self-motivated, children's own inner sense of a need to learn, achieve and grow

Parents – used generally, could be single parent, primary care giver, foster parent and not just the biological parent

Pedagogy – the way that we teach children as early childhood educators

Portage – a specialist home visiting and education programme for children with special educational needs

Portfolio – a personal file which includes all the student's evidence of learning and achievement: documents, papers, notes, photographs, children's work, etc.

Provision – what is provided in nurseries for young children to use and explore

Schemas – patterns of linked behaviours which the child can generalise and use in a whole variety of different situations

Sensitive period – this term refers to both the plasticity of the brain during the early years, when it seems most likely to adapt to new situations, and to the equally significant role of the environment, in shaping attitudes and values

Sequence of photographs – a set of photographs taken while a child is engaged in one activity, showing what happened. They might be taken during a few seconds or over a longer period of time

Training Programme – nursery nursing course, NVQ programme, or other childcare course

Transition – the movement from one environment to another, such as from home to nursery

Treasure baskets – developed by Elinor Goldschmied. Baskets containing natural objects of interest to babies and toddlers

Visual aid – some sort of representation that can be seen and is used to aid understanding

Index